Advanced Praise for A

"Dawn's story reminds us that CliftonStrengths® coaching is both science and art. Through understanding and harnessing her strengths and those of Daran's, Dawn created a customized plan for his recovery — proving there is no limit to what is possible. Their story is pure inspiration."

Jim Clifton
Chairman and CEO of Gallup, Inc.
Author of *It's the Manager,* #1 *Wall Street Journal* bestseller

---

"God has a purpose for us. Your skills, talent, and knowledge are His. In her book, *ARMORED*, Dawn reveals her story about how her faith was strengthened through life-threatening trials as she was a care coach for her husband. Leveraging her God-Given Gifts, she conquered those battles and is now using her testimony to be an inspiration to others. She inspired me as I am a caregiver, too, in a situation that I never would have suspected with my daughter. This book will continue to be a place for me to go for encouragement."

Diane Paddison
Founder and Executive Director of 4word, Author of *Work, Love, Pray and Be Refreshed . . . a year of devotions for women in the workplace*
Former Global Executive Team of two Fortune 500 and one Fortune 1000 companies

"As a 25-year healthcare professional and now executive leader, I often see how caregivers struggle to forge a path of how best to play their role. Dawn combines her great business coaching skills in helping organizations navigate complexity to forge a pathway through, along with her newly acquired skills of being a care coach. The wisdom Dawn confluences from these two sides of her life is refreshing and compelling. I think business coaches can draw lessons from it and caregivers would be refreshed and inspired by it."

Chris Comeaux
President/CEO
Teleios Collaborative Network

"As a mental health professional, I work with clients as they tread through life's unfavorable challenges. Rarely are they prepared for the arduous, severe, and faith-testing situations they encounter. I agree with Dawn as she writes in *ARMORED*, you have to stay in focus and leverage every experience, no matter how ill-prepared or attacked by adversity you feel. Dawn shares her story and insights in a truly authentic, humorous, yet extraordinarily powerful way that will guide and support anyone trying to 'armor up' and conquer their own battles."

Tiffany C. Moreno
Licensed Professional Counselor
National Board of Certified Counselors

"Dawn's vulnerable story of finding strength as an advocate and overcomer is truly refreshing. Her faith in God releases the role of care coach, and every reader will be able to relate in some way to her journey while gaining new insight."

Laura Wilcox
Sacred Story Ministries Executive Director
and Author of *Capture My Heart, Lord*

"We've all been in situations when things didn't go as planned, but what happens when that unexpected turn of events instantly thrusts you into a critical caregiver role where you feel totally unprepared and unqualified to fill? In *ARMORED*, Dawn beautifully shares her personal struggles, experiences, and revelations as she unintentionally stepped into the full-time role as the primary caregiver to her husband over three life-threatening illnesses. Her expertise and down to earth humor will inspire you and give you practical advice and strategies to help you grow into and cherish your newfound opportunity to serve; not just as the caregiver, but as the care coach!"

Michelle Prince
Best-Selling Author, Speaker & CEO
Performance Publishing Group

ARMORED

May God Bless and Keep You Now and Always!

Gen. F. Lindsey

ARMORED

A Memoir
with Inspirational and Practical Life Strategies

by

Dawn F. Landry

Authentizity, LLC.
Houston, Texas
2020

Paperback: ISBN 978-1-7353540-3-3
Hard Cover: ISBN 978-1-7353540-0-2
eBook: ISBN 978-1-7353540-2-6

Library of Congress Control Number: 2020912756

Book design by Markind, LLC
Front cover and graphics by House Atlantic Media, LLC
Editing by O'Neil Resources, LLC
All photographs by Dawn F. Landry unless otherwise credited

Printed and bound in USA
First Edition: 2020

Authentizity, LLC.
Houston, Texas, USA
www.authentizity.com

Visit www.dawnflandry.com

Dedication

This book is dedicated to my husband, Daran Ray Landry. Thank you for choosing me first, for believing in me long before I believed in myself, and for showing me that true, everlasting, unfailing love exists. I will always nurture and go to battle for our love, regardless of what life throws at us because I believe and have witnessed how miracles are possible when the two of us surrender to God.

This photo was taken of Daran and me in 2010, several months following his cancer battle. While we survived several trials in the years prior, the most challenging testing and endurance of our faith and strength were yet to come.

Contents

Introduction

I do not know what it is like to hear the words, "You have cancer." I have never had an entire side of my body paralyzed nor been incapable of speaking.

I have been a bystander during these unimaginable events as they struck the person that I love most in the world — my husband, Daran Landry. While I have witnessed and walked beside Daran every step of the way as he has overcome seemingly insurmountable obstacles, my experience is still secondhand. The thoughts collected in this book are from my perspective as his biggest advocate and cheerleader. I have not, nor will I ever, claim to know what he has felt as the patient.

My story, as I detail it here, is as real and raw as it gets. I make no pretenses, nor do I sugarcoat any of it. I am *especially* neither a healthcare professional nor extremely maternal for that matter. Additionally, I'm not an idle, sit still, and be a bystander kind of person. Call me driven, but I always need to have a purpose and feel useful. I am a determined planner with a quirky, self-deprecating sense of humor, a strategic mind, and a unique approach to conquering challenges. Most of all, I have a deep, steadfast faith that God will see us through. And while I may like to have my *Dawn* plan, I am neither rigid nor unadaptable. Thank goodness for that because God has a funny sense of humor and likes to see how fast I can bend and transform!

In characterizing some of my life the past twenty years, you might call me an "unexpected caregiver," since every illness that afflicted Daran came as a surprise, sneak attack. Although I have never felt like the noun *caregiver* adequately described me, nor how I served him. As someone comfortable being a *big dreamer*, unconventional, and naturally curious, I pressed myself further to explore why. By the way, did you know that the term *caregiver* is used mainly in the United States, Canada, and China; while the UK, Australia, and other European countries use *carer* as a moniker for these activities? Researching and discovering this further validated to me that all of us have the freedom to call ourselves whatever we choose whenever we're in battle situations.

I recently asked Daran what he thought about the label *caregiver* as it related to me. He chuckled and agreed that I am not a *caregiver* in the conventional use of the word. He also said that the traditional form of caregiving would not have worked for him anyway. He doesn't respond well to the usual forms of mothering, smothering, or quite frankly, being treated like a patient.

You see, the way our partnership works is more like that of battle-tested soldiers who know one another so well that they become an extension of each other, like another appendage. Since *caregiver* doesn't fit as a description of the role that I played in Daran's recovery, I searched to find a better word. I settled on the name *care coach*. It is a better measure of who I am and what I do.

Care coaching allowed me to have a role in Daran's recovery in my own, nontraditional way. This surprised many of his doctors, nurses, and therapists, and they told me that they have never seen anyone be present for their loved one in this manner.

My definition of a care coach still encompasses the conventionally ascribed aspects of care. However, it is more personalized, individualized, and includes deep love, devotion, compassion, and respect. Care coaching also entails much more such as being an advocate, providing hope, reminding the patient of who they are and what they are fighting for, as well as being a strong supporter through the most challenging of times. Most of all, care coaching is about lovingly motivating the patient through their battles with unwavering faith.

My brand of care was not intentional, it was innate and authentic. It encompassed all my past experiences, which unwittingly prepared me for these battles. Cumulatively, I was armored, both spiritually and physically, to utilize my strengths and to encourage Daran by tapping into his strengths.

I have abstractedly incorporated battle terminology in both the title and contents of this book. That is deliberate. Ephesians 6:11-18 is my *go-to* Bible verse. I am a visual learner and this verse serves as a graphical reminder for me that we are to be an active participant in armoring up for any battles that we face.

God equipped me in my own unique way for these battles; the same is true for Daran. As part of armoring up, I strategically and creatively used my personal strengths to develop patient-centric activities that placed Daran at the epicenter of all decisions and actions. These endeavors met us at our respective comfort levels of experience, talents, passions, and preferences.

[11] Put on the whole armour of God, that ye may be able to stand against the wiles of the devil.

[12] For we wrestle not against flesh and blood, but against principalities, against powers, against the rulers of the darkness of this world, against spiritual wickedness in high places.

[13] Wherefore take unto you the whole armour of God, that ye may be able to withstand in the evil day, and having done all, to stand.

[14] Stand therefore, having your loins girt about with truth, and having on the breastplate of righteousness;

[15] And your feet shod with the preparation of the gospel of peace;

[16] Above all, taking the shield of faith, wherewith ye shall be able to quench all the fiery darts of the wicked.

[17] And take the helmet of salvation, and the sword of the Spirit, which is the word of God:

[18] Praying always with all prayer and supplication in the Spirit and watching thereunto with all perseverance and supplication for all saints.

EPHESIANS 6:11-18 (KJV)

In the early chapters of this book, I will detail who we are as individuals and as partners to provide the context for the later chapters which define Daran's health battles. At the conclusion of each chapter, I will share strategies, insights, tactics, and advice from the lessons I learned. I will then offer a care coach question for you to consider. In the final chapters of the book, you'll find a summary of my Top 10 Battle Strategies, along with my Gratitude Journey and *Lagniappe*, or a little something extra. (Note: We are both native Louisianians; I use Cajun terminology throughout the book to personalize it to us, in jest, and as emphasis of our backgrounds.)

What were the common themes from my care coaching experiences; what were the shining moments that prevailed? Our Unfailing God, Daran's warrior spirit, our mutual tenacity, and our abiding love for one another were a nice, well-mixed gumbo that successfully got us through it all.

My goal in telling our story is that you will be inspired, no matter your caregiving (or care coaching) background or skill set, and understand that we all have the power within us to encourage our loved ones through the darkest of times in life's medical journeys.

As a care coach equipped with only the armor of my unique past experiences, if I can motivate and support the person that I love most in the world through three major, life-threatening illnesses, then you can too.

CHAPTER
ONE

My Story
— Surrendered to Serve

Big Dreamer

I'm a gal who was, and still is, a *big dreamer*. By general stereotypes and outward observations, I should never have achieved the successes that I can blessedly claim today. I don't come from wealth or connections, but by the Grace of God and a lot of hard work, I have surpassed my childhood fantasies for a beautiful life with a wonderful, loving husband and rewarding career.

I grew up in the 1970s in a small, rural town in south Louisiana. We lived modestly on my father's plumbing company income; mom was a housewife, who also handled his financial books.

My earliest memories are of my father's explosive temper. Later in his life, his mental instability was diagnosed as bipolar schizophrenia; but in my childhood, it manifested in physical abuse, as well as his emotionally and verbally toxic words to my mom, my brothers, my sister, and me.

During those early and formative years, my respite was in the company and the influence of my maternal grandparents. As the oldest of four children, their house was my refuge that ensured solitude and creativity. It also fueled my curiosity and imagination.

My grandmother doted on me, while my grandfather planted seeds of greatness inside of me. He was a self-made, self-educated, informed man with a voracious appetite for reading anything and everything he could get his hands on. Their living room was filled with volumes of encyclopedias, endless copies of *Reader's Digest* magazines, and books that detailed stories of other people's interesting lives and faraway, exotic places.

My grandfather worked for the same company his entire career and ascended the corporate ladder from a factory line worker to head foreman in a carbon black plant. He was a natural-born leader. His work ethic was solid and enviable in that he rose each day at 3:30 a.m. to ensure his timely arrival at work by 5:00 a.m. He was always predictably early.

He was a big man with a booming, welcoming voice, who drew others to him. I can still hear his greeting of "Hello there!" and his contagious, deep laugh, as well as feel his full-on barrel hugs. He was my role model and my biggest advocate. He passed away a year before seeing me graduate from college and begin a successful career of my own.

King or Kingmaker?

"Are you a king or a kingmaker?" I remember that question just like it was yesterday — even though it was asked over 30 years ago. It was early in my college courses, and the question was posed by my professor in Public Relations 101. She explained, "If you are a king, then a career in public relations is likely the wrong field for you. Truly great public relations professionals are kingmakers."

Through the years, I have had some slight dabbles in the spotlight. However, I've never wanted to be king. I am confidently a kingmaker. As I will detail later in this book, I awaken each morning and ask, *God who can I serve today?*

I've spent over twenty-seven years as a business executive, singularly driven to advance in my profession. In the early part of my career when I was in my twenties and early-to-mid thirties, you might define me as restless and impatient. Things weren't happening fast enough for me, so I'd move on to the next job within a couple of years, which was completely counter to my grandfather's model.

Eventually, I found my home in Houston's corporate real estate industry, excelling in business development and marketing leadership positions within the region's largest economic development organization, as well as international commercial construction companies.

And just when I thought that I had settled in and had things figured out, God allowed another growth opportunity to press and stretch me to the next level. In February 2017, I founded Authentizity, LLC, as an independent business growth strategist to assist companies with customized programs designed to advance their leadership proficiencies, team alignment, and outreach effectiveness. I became a Gallup-Certified CliftonStrengths® Coach and then leveraged that tool to provide consulting, training, and coaching services that optimize technical teams' engagement and productivity.

Even with *big dreams,* I have experienced the harsh realities of my self-limiting and self-imposed roadblocks. However, I have also witnessed that, if I open myself to growth, I will be challenged and step up to the task before me.

Self-Improvement and Advancement Driven

To get to where I am today, I have worked hard at self-awareness and improvement. Basically, I redirected my innate curiosity internally towards myself. I am a work in progress. I know that I am nowhere near where I am going to be. However, I am also eons from where I started.

I speak from experience when I state that before I did the work in self-reflection and naval gazing — including the time, resource, and financial investment — I was very much frustrated and was frustrating to many around me.

Through the past thirty years, I have read many self-help books, completed countless personality tests and supporting workbooks, and taken several self-improvement courses. They have all added to the mosaic of who I have become. Yet, the Simon Sinek WHY Discovery and Gallup CliftonStrengths® assessment activities are the two that have influenced me the most to date.

Purpose Discovery

Knowing and articulating your "WHY", as defined by internationally-acclaimed Simon Sinek, has become a popular movement over the past decade; and that's a good thing. As he explains, if you don't know the reason why you get up in the morning, then how can you communicate the value that you bring?

Sinek gained mass public attention following his first Ted Talk in 2009. Since that time, he has inspired millions around the globe by sharing his visionary thinking in his speeches, coaching, and bestselling books.

After reading and watching Sinek, I so agreed with these concepts that I participated in a three-day WHY Discovery workshop in October of 2017. I soon learned that what I thought was my WHY was really one of my HOWs and that my WHY was something completely different. Sinek teaches that: "for a WHY to be a good WHY its foundation must be in service to others; it must be in the present tense; it must be inspirational, not aspirational." (Note: Sinek capitalizes these words throughout his teachings for emphasis.)

Once I had honed my own WHY my past decisions began to make more sense to me. Defining my WHY has also served as a gauge for my future decisions.

My "WHY" is:

- To Inspire, Ignite, and Activate the Greatness in Others and Myself.

My "HOWs" are:

- To Invest in Others.
- To Be a Resource.
- To Identify and Articulate Value to Others and Myself.
- To Collect/Deliver the Right Information and People at the Right Time.
- To Live a Life of Independence and Excellence.
- To Move Forward and Surrender to the Possibilities of the Future.
- To Stay Disciplined and Continue to Work Hard.

Besides knowing my WHY and HOWs, it has also been extremely valuable to understand my strengths. To briefly explain the importance of understanding individual strengths, CliftonStrengths Finder is a psychological assessment based upon decades of research and refinement by Gallup, Inc. The assessment was founded by Don Clifton, an American psychologist, educator, author, researcher, and entrepreneur.

Whether used personally or professionally, studies have shown that with awareness of our own CliftonStrengths Finder results, individuals and teams create a common language, empathy, and appreciation of the worth of each person's respective talents. Rather than concentrating on our weaknesses, CliftonStrengths Finder asks us to embrace who we are and operate from the areas in which we are strongest and most engaged. It acknowledges our strengths as our superpowers and encourages us to proactively and positively lean on our fellow partners to advance our mission and vision. (Note: I will provide much more detail about this topic in Chapter Four, and in the Reference and *Lagniappe* Section later in the book.)

Cumulatively, knowledge of my WHY, HOWs, and CliftonStrengths propels me forward. I realize that, by embracing my uniqueness, I show up as my true, authentic self.

Self-Guiding Principle Development

By channeling my internal compass, through the years I have developed self-guiding principles that drive my decisions.

I choose to live a life in which I stand in forgiveness. C.S. Lewis said, "To be a Christian means to forgive the inexcusable because God has forgiven the inexcusable in you." This is never easy, especially when you are called to forgive someone who was supposed to love you unconditionally from birth.

Rather than live in the past as a victim, I chose a long time ago to hold myself accountable for my own joy and future fate. Just as the Bible promises, forgiveness is an amazing healer. I know because over twenty years ago I made the choice to forgive my dad for all the pain he caused my family and me. When I did, I became free.

To me, freedom means being present in your current life circumstances. It also means owning who you are, warts and all, with a sense of peace and contentment for today.

I choose to live a life in which I stand in authenticity. I value this principle so passionately that I named my company, Authentizity.

What does living authentically mean to me? It means being your true self in public and in private, without false airs or pretense. It is being transparent and direct; not mean, but honest. Most of all, it is leveraging one's self-awareness to create boundaries, or bumper guards, for how you allow others to treat you.

I choose to live a life in which I stand in servitude. In 2009, when Daran was enduring one of the fights for his life, I began asking for *manna* (i.e., provision) for the day. I also started a morning ritual, first thing before my feet hit the floor, of asking, "God, who can I serve today?"

I aspire to serve as best I can, starting in the morning and then thanking God at the end of the day. I find that my days are a lot happier when I take my ego out of the equation and live to serve.

My God Journey

My walk with God has not been in a straight line. I was raised with a strong, Catholic upbringing, and I was a good girl and rule follower that obeyed out of obligation. While I respect Catholicism's traditions because they remind me of my grandmother, the doctrine never fully took root in me. So, in my late teens and well into my twenties, I veered away from practicing any faith.

During that time, I didn't consider myself a non-believer and I was definitely not an atheist. It was more that I was distracted with life and self-absorbed so my walk was far away from God. Occasionally throughout those years, I would notice the breadcrumbs that He continued to leave for me. I now realize that God was always there to protect me, even when I know that I disappointed Him. I now consider myself a non-denominational Christian and seeker of God's Word and His Gospel.

When Daran and I were first dating, we sought a church in which we were both fed spiritually. Through the years, and in the many cities in which we lived, we attended no fewer than twenty churches. We wanted to explore different Christian-based denominations. We found our church home in 2004 in Lakewood Church. We first began by watching Pastor Joel Osteen on television. In June of 2005, when Lakewood opened the new church in the central part of Houston, we attended that first night. Since then, we have considered ourselves members. Over the years, my understanding of the Bible has grown, as has my pursuit of a walk closer to God, His Son, Jesus Christ, and the Holy Spirit.

I know that, without a strong faith, I would not have survived the battles that these past two decades have brought Daran and me. Through my surrender to His Path, I have emotionally survived to write about it.

♔ Key Battle Strategy

Through self-awareness and introspection, I know myself and have invested in difficult self-development through stretching and pressing to improve.

_____

_____

_____

_____

_____

♔ Care Coach Question

In which areas of your life, can you focus your efforts towards forgiveness, surrender, and authenticity to advance your capabilities?

_____

_____

_____

_____

This photo was taken in Lafayette, Louisiana when I was twenty-seven years old. While still early in my career, I was determined to make an impact both professionally and personally in life.

Always naturally self-reflective, I am especially introspective when on vacation. This photo was taken in 2013 while we visited San Juan, Puerto Rico.

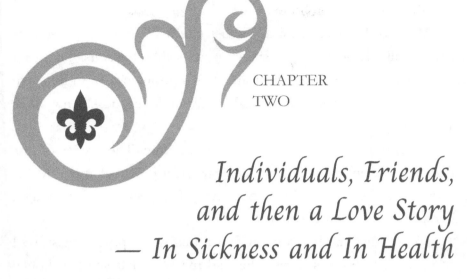

Individuals, Friends, and then a Love Story — In Sickness and In Health

"Single in the City" Dawn

There is a lyric in a Garth Brooks' song that says, "Some of God's Greatest Gifts are unanswered prayers." If ever there was a synopsis of how Daran and I came together, then that's how I would describe it.

Throughout my early to mid-twenties, I was lost with little-to-no self-esteem. This was projected outwardly to the types of men that I was interested in and that were attracted to me. I didn't know who I was, nor did I love myself. How in the world could I be a good, healthy partner in a relationship?

The turning point for me came in June of 1996 when a two-and-a-half-year, emotionally abusive relationship with a guy that I'll call "Mr. Toxic" crumbled. Mr. Toxic was ego-driven, and I was his trophy. He took pleasure in demeaning me verbally to make himself feel better and to keep me in my place. He would often introduce me this way: "Meet Dawn Marie. I picked her up on the side of the road and she didn't have any shoes on."

Mr. Toxic wasn't physically abusive, but his words and actions emotionally depleted me in every way possible. Let's just say that I knew that I was near rock bottom when a phone call from him sent me into a spiral so bad that I found myself under my desk in my office at work!

I was working at an ad agency at the time. The owner of the firm was a phenomenal mentor and saw great potential in me. As my supervisor, she invested in me personally. I respected her and sought her advice and counsel often.

I knew that she had a good friend that was a psychologist, so I asked for her friend's name. She told me later that she had hoped that I'd do so because she saw me struggling. Instead of offering the referral to me, she decided to wait until I was ready to ask for help. I was twenty-eight years old by then and had never dealt with the many issues stemming from my childhood. Basically, I had "looked for love in all the wrong places." Yep, that's another country song!

I remember the cost for the psychologist like it was yesterday — $75.00 per hour in 1998. The psychologist didn't accept insurance. Since I was on an extremely tight budget, I tried to schedule an appointment at least two to three times per month. In retrospect, that was the best money that I ever spent on myself. I would do it all over again and then some!

There are so many nuggets of wisdom that I carry with me over twenty years later; I know that my life is forever changed by taking that time and space to identify who I was. In those appointments, I went from dreaming to defining the future which included who I was then, and who I envisioned becoming.

For example, my psychologist told me that I must learn to find a way to deal with the common personality types from the individuals that I struggled with in my twenties. Otherwise, they would return in my thirties, forties, and the rest of my life, just in different people. With my continual people-pleasing, cowering, shutting down, and not establishing boundaries for myself, I might lead a less than fulfilled and oftentimes self-abusive life.

My psychologist also asked that I compile a list of the top characteristics that I sought in a partner. I sat down and began writing. Once completed, it contained fifty-two items. At the top of that list was "Must Believe in God." Having dated two self-proclaimed atheists (including Mr. Toxic), I knew that was the biggest deal-breaker for me. There were also other *must-have* ones encompassing how I wanted my future partner to respect and treat me. Don't get me wrong, there were some superficial items as well, but I always knew that those were less important in the grand scheme of things.

Once I had *The List,* I did little to no dating of substance, and many didn't make it to a second date. When I did date, it wasn't long-lasting because I hadn't fully worked through my father issues and hadn't forgiven him yet. I also wasn't clear on who I was or what I wanted. Although the clarity was slowly forming, and I was finally beginning to recognize what I could healthily contribute to a relationship.

At the time, the HBO series, *Sex and the City* had just been released. Like the sisterhood represented on the show, I was part of a small group of single, late twenties, career-minded girlfriends. We gathered for lunch each Friday to share our weekly work triumphs and to discuss our dating lives.

Once I had created *The List* for my future partner, my friends would tease me every time I rejected yet another candidate after the first date. They joked about the length of *The List*, as if it were this massively, heavy book that they were trying to set on the restaurant dining table.

Deep down, I knew that I wasn't dreaming too big and boldly; little did I know that my guy was right under my nose the whole time!

Segue to Daran

Daran chose me, at first...

He can tell you what I was wearing the first time he met me, January of 1996, at a Lafayette Chamber of Commerce event. I don't recall meeting him for another six months.

Recovering from the hurt of a cheating girlfriend, Daran had just moved back to Lafayette from Dallas. Because some of Daran's family graduated from high school with Mr. Toxic (who I was still with at the time), Daran knew of him and his reputation. When he found out that I was dating Mr. Toxic, Daran predicted that it wouldn't last, so he stayed in touch.

Daran and I worked in parallel industries; he was in sales at a trade show design and marketing firm and I was at the ad agency. I became his client. We shared common accounts, and even networked to brainstorm new client opportunities. Our relationship evolved into a great, platonic friendship lasting more than three years.

It's not that Daran isn't a handsomely attractive man, but for whatever reason, I had blinders on and couldn't see him any other way than as a friend. In hindsight, I know that I wasn't fully ready for a mature and secure relationship. Being the amazing man that he is, Daran waited.

20 ✤

That doesn't mean that he was a monk, though! While waiting for me, he dated, sometimes in longer-term relationships, but he later told me that those were never serious. He was just holding out for me. Crazy, right?

I hate to admit it, but even when Daran's affection was directly pointed out to me, I couldn't see it. One day I attended the Lafayette business expo at the Cajundome and was walking around with one of my best friends. It's a relatively small town, so many of us in the business community knew one another. Daran was working at his company's booth, so we stopped by to say hello. After we walked away, she said, "He has it bad for you." Perplexed, I questioned her, "Daran? Daran Landry? No; he talks to all the girls that way."

The three of us laugh about that exchange to this day. Daran swears that he didn't talk to girls that way; I was just that clueless!

Other similar incidents occurred, but again, I wasn't ready. That all changed when Daran moved to New Orleans to open a new office for his employer — only then did I realize how much I missed his presence. We soon began a regular, Friday afternoon practice of ending our work week with a conference call to recap our week's activities. No subject was off-limits and our conversations encompassed professional, as well as personal topics.

The theme "absence makes the heart grow fonder" became a part of our story, too. You can probably predict what happens next, but I'll tell you any way…

Several months went by without us seeing one another. One day Daran called me to tell me that he was coming to Lafayette to be a part of a client event occurring the following week. His company was hosting a trade show manufacturer from Europe. They were having a big crawfish boil at his boss's house that Tuesday and Daran asked if I would attend with him.

I thought I was his *work date*. Why wouldn't I? I was a great work date — I was a business professional, and I knew how to dress the part. I could carry an interesting conversation, even enduring the dullest of small talk, and I wouldn't embarrass him. I would even positively augment his work efforts.

We enjoyed a lovely evening. After Daran and I left his event, I asked him if he owned a tuxedo. While this wasn't my typical topic of conversation after a messy crawfish boil, I inquired about this because I had learned earlier that day that my date for that Friday night's Bishop's Charity Ball, an event in which I was leading the Public Relations, was unable to attend.

Daran told me that he did have a tuxedo, but I later learned that he had lied. At the time, he was bodybuilding and couldn't find a tux that fit properly over his biceps or barrel chest. So this crazy, sweet guy drove to Baton Rouge (nearly sixty miles away) and had a custom one made in less than two days. To this day, he has never told me how much that cost him.

The Ball was wonderful, and it ended early, so we rented a movie and went back to my apartment. While watching the movie, I fell asleep on the floor in the living room; so he quietly left. Just before I so rudely began snoozing, though, he asked me to go boating with him, his roommate, and his roommate's girlfriend that Sunday.

That Sunday culminated our week of dates — each completely distinct than the last yet revealing different sides and commonalities of our respective personalities. I love being on any body of open water; peace and contentment envelopes me. Daran had never seen that side of me. We had a great day in the sun, gliding down the bayou with the bright sky above us. At the end of the day, Daran kissed me for the first time. Up until that time, he was a complete gentleman and hadn't made a move. He now teases me about how bad I was at dating, especially when I recall that I didn't know we were dating until the third date!

That's when I chose him, and we've been inseparable ever since.

Dawn and Daran, the Love Story

Even as I write this, I must admit that I know our love story is so saccharine and mushy. I mean, really. Does this kind of thing really happen? Yes, it does. It is one hundred percent real and inspiring, even to me.

Once my eyes were opened, I allowed my brain to evolve my image of Daran as a phenomenal friend to Daran as my boyfriend. When I did that, I began reflecting on *The List*. As I recalled Daran's many attributes, I realized that he had all but two of the characteristics that I had listed years before. Neither of those was a deal-breaker, and most importantly Daran checked my number one with his love of, and strong faith in God.

Daran is truer to his commitments than any person that I've ever met. Daran's word is his bond. For instance, at thirteen years old, he wrote in his Bible during a summer Bible Camp that he would never drink. He has kept to his word even to this day despite intense peer pressure from family and friends. They could never sway him. I surmised that if he made a commitment to me, then he'd keep it.

Even with all the self-improvement work that I had done on myself, when I was confronted with a mature relationship with a wonderful man, I was still unsure. The ghosts of my past still haunted me. Early in our relationship, I even tried to talk Daran out of dating me because I wasn't used to anyone treating me so well. We now laugh how I even quoted books about how I didn't deserve him. He never wavered, and I slowly became comfortable with Daran's kindness and respect for me.

Somewhere along the way (perhaps it was from my psychologist), I learned that by observing the familial relationships of your partner, you may witness how you will be treated. When we were dating, I noticed how well Daran's dad treated his mom. Having been born into a highly dysfunctional and physically, emotionally, and verbally abusive parental relationship that ultimately ended in divorce, I observed Daran's family very closely. I knew that if Daran was raised to witness an emotionally healthy couple, then he was more likely to emulate that behavior. As I grew more and more confident in the love we shared, my defenses fell one by one and I allowed myself to fully embrace our life together.

And here is where you would predict that I would say: "And they lived happily ever after…"

Challenges, But in Lock Step

In actuality, we had a lot of life occur between our first date in April 1999 and our wedding day five years later. Early on we struggled financially, but always had love, a roof over our heads, food to eat, and laughter to lighten our spirits through life's challenges. We share an appreciation for travel and curiosity to experience new cultures, so we moved to Dallas and then to San Francisco in search of new adventures.

In 2001, we experienced much loss. His dad and my grandmother died within a month of one another just weeks following the 911 attacks. In our mutual mourning, we realized that voyages were good, but we needed to live closer to our families in Louisiana. We settled in Houston in the latter part of that year.

During this time, our careers were evolving to be more closely aligned with our experiences and passions. We always supported one another in our commitments to work and climbing our respective corporate ladders.

Children were never an option for me. I was diagnosed with endometriosis at age seventeen and, by thirty-five, I had endured two laparoscopies and, eventually, a hysterectomy. In my nature, I'm not very maternal; I gravitate more towards puppies over babies, so the *no kid* choice was acceptable to me. None of this was a surprise to Daran since I was transparent about my health issues, even when we were platonic friends. Fortunately, this didn't dissuade him.

With so much life packed into that time, there was no pressure concerning marriage because we felt like true partners already. We had been living together for a couple of years and were visiting Daran's paternal grandmother. In a moment when she was alone with me, she asked me about any marriage plans that we might have. I told her that I would never give Daran an ultimatum; that just wasn't true to our relationship. I told her that, when Daran proposed, it would mean that he was ready.

When it did occur, the day was unexpectedly average. Daran's proposal wasn't romantic; and yet it was typical for our relationship. I was on the phone with him at the end of a normal workday. I was in the middle of a project and told him that I'd be at work a while longer. I could tell that he was stressed out, so I asked him why. It was December, and I wasn't surprised to hear that he had been delivering Christmas gifts to clients all day. That didn't seem so stressful to me, and I told him so.

He said that wasn't the reason for his anxiety. Rather, in between his deliveries, he was shopping for engagement rings. He didn't know what kind I would like, so he told me that I'd have to select my own. I said, "What?" He repeated that I would have to accompany him to the store and choose my own. I then said, "Huh?" and "What?" about three more times.

He then replied, "Would you please stop saying 'huh' and 'what'?!" Yep, that is exactly how he proposed.

As I retell the story about how Daran proposed over the phone, some people have asked if he was serving in a war or traveling far from home for business. I laugh and tell them how even his proposal reflects how we collaborate as partners and problem-solvers in everything!

Our Big, Fat Cajun Wedding

After all that time as platonic friends, you might ask, why did Daran finally ask me out on that first date?

Let me remind you that I am a *big dreamer*. At that point in my life, I was in my late twenties, restless, and ready to see the world. I felt that I had been holding myself back by continuing to live in my home state, near my hometown. Additionally, I was burnt out in my career, having pushed myself on several large, high profile, public relations projects.

While on one of our Friday afternoon calls, I expressed to Daran that I was thinking about selling everything that I owned and moving to Greece. Now I had never been to Greece, nor did I know anyone who lived there. I simply had always been fascinated with that country. I was dreaming, but Daran took me seriously.

In hindsight, I can't believe how convincing I was! In his mind, this was his last chance to ask me out. He rationalized it as, "What do I have to lose? She's going to move to a different continent anyway. If I don't ask her, she's going to be gone and I will never have asked her out."

And so that was the catalyst for the beginning of our dating relationship, with a Greek theme intricately woven into it.

Once Daran proposed, I suggested that we marry on the island of Santorini, Greece. He agreed.

However, there was a problem. Neither of our moms likes to fly, and my mom is deathly afraid of water. We tried to negotiate with them, suggesting that we'd fly there, get married, and come back and have a big party. That wasn't acceptable. We then suggested that we'd fly there, get married, and come back, reenact it, and have a big party. Still no good. Finally, we realized that it was too much to do both. That's when our *Big, Fat Greek Wedding* became our *Big, Fat Cajun Wedding*!

Our wedding was simple but beautiful. It was held outside in Lafayette, Louisiana, at a Cajun historic preservation venue called Acadian Village, on a sweltering, humid evening. In Cajun French, we'd describe it as *ça fait chaud*, which translates as "it is hot!" Thinking back on it, though, I wouldn't change a thing.

Randy, my mom's younger brother, gave me away. Even though I don't call him Uncle Randy, I've always been extremely bonded to him, and having him as my escort down the aisle just felt right. Holly, my only sister, was maid of honor, and Daran's "uncle brother",

Scotty, was the best man. Scotty is Daran's dad's youngest brother. Daran and Scotty are only one and a half years apart in age and grew up like brothers.

Besides our moms, these three phenomenal human beings would become the unique threads knit into our life story then, now, and forevermore. There were many family members and friends who also were there to celebrate our love that unfortunately are no longer with us. This makes that day especially frozen in time in my memory as one of the best days of my life surrounded by the people who meant the most to me.

And, if there was a theme for our wedding, it was clearly expressed in the toasts made at our reception. You could summarize it this way: "It was about damn time!"

For our week-long honeymoon, we flew to a small island off Cancun named Isla Mujeres. It was then that we realized that, while we had moved to several locations throughout the country, we had never vacationed together just for enjoyment and entertainment. While still in Mexico, we made a pact that instead of exchanging anniversary gifts, we would celebrate our love by taking an annual trip. That week is as much a treasure of time as it is of travel. It enables us to reset, reconnect, and honor our love and commitment to one another.

Through the years, that dream of going to Greece never faltered, it only became stronger. In fact, we planned that trip several other times unsuccessfully before we finally traveled there for our fifteen-year anniversary in the Spring of 2019. We took a cruise, sailing out of Rome to visit Athens and four Greek Islands, including Santorini. While on Santorini, we visited the scenic town of Oia, where we renewed our vows in front of a beautiful, old, blue-roofed church.

The entire trip was romantic and magical *and* most definitely worth the wait!

Keep On Keeping On

In the years after our marriage, Daran and I slowly excelled in our careers and developed a routine.

Houston truly became our home and our respective relationships, work and personal, grew to encompass a vast and varied network of friends who have become family. We cherish them as Divine Connections, God-Ordained.

As we were creating and maintaining these friendships by just doing and being who we are, there was no way for us to have known how important these connections would be in the difficult years ahead. There are many times in Daran's illnesses when I could feel our friends and family spiritually and physically propping us up in full support, enabling us to keep going.

Early in our marriage, we were surprised to learn that Daran had a son he knew nothing about. His son was sixteen years old at the time we learned of his existence.

At first, their relationship was more like that of an uncle and nephew. However, it has evolved over time into a true father and son bond. His son is now a few years older than Daran was when Daran and I began dating. His son resembles Daran at that age; he even has some of Daran's mannerisms and unique preferences in food choices. That took me aback at first; it's clearly nature versus nurture at work.

Their relationship has been beautiful to observe as it's a gift that I could never have given Daran. I love the way the two of them handled the entire situation, coming together and loving one another in a mature and healthy way.

We are gratified that our family continues to grow around us as through God's Grace they bring us joy and enrich our lives in so many countless ways. We are surrounded by this amazing army that shares our lives in sickness and in health.

Speaking of health, I would be remiss if I didn't especially highlight this aspect of who we are. Throughout my life, I have always eaten clean and taken care of myself. I have been a pescatarian since I was seventeen years old and, in my late thirties, I found out that I was gluten intolerant. Additionally, I stay active by doing Pilates and going to the gym. However, in no way can I compare to the health extremist that is Daran Ray Landry.

Daran's commitment to his workouts is what some might deem extreme. It's not that he's obsessive, it's just that he has been a gym rat since a very young age. It's his social hour, and he welcomes the endorphin rush of a great workout. He knows how to push his body to its maximum to achieve his desired results, and he loves the soreness that he feels from his tired muscles afterward.

He *loves* the gym because it not only challenges his inner strength physically in building his body, but it also develops his mind and spirit. While the normal person, present company included, can endure a workout of an hour or so a few days a week, Daran's average workout has been two to three hours, six to seven days per week for more than thirty years. Although — and he'll rib me for saying so — he does exercise his jaw in various conversations during his gym time. When he enters the gym, it's always a welcome homecoming with the regulars who fondly call him "Coach."

In those first few years of being together, we spent a lot of time at the gym. It's where we fell in love most. He liked training me and demonstrating his knowledge of health and kinesiology. It's his passion. He's also a trained paramedic, even though he has never practiced as one.

That love of well-being also translated to meal prep. He has a routine of grilling large volumes of skinless, boneless chicken breasts each Sunday for the upcoming week. Daran can eat the same meal over and again and never get tired of it! As I mentioned earlier, he doesn't drink, nor has he ever smoked or done drugs.

I state all of this as a precursor to indicate that he was following all the rules. Surely, he should be a pillar of great health, right?

In Sickness and In Health

Traditional wedding vows state, "...in sickness and in health." I often advise the young adults in my life that this is a reminder that their choices for future partners matter. When you're young, in a relationship, and healthy, you can never fully anticipate what life has in store for your separate but intertwined journeys together.

Physical appearances and amorous sex fade over time, no matter the relationship. In the depths of *real life*, you'd better really like that person *a lot*. That is because life will often get tough and your partner may become unexpectedly ill requiring you to push yourself to do things that are heartbreaking, challenging, and beyond anything that you feel prepared for.

And when it gets hard, you keep marching forward. Do you know why? It's not because they would do the same for you, even though they would. You keep going because you don't have a choice — that is *your person* lying in that bed and you would give them the world, change places with them if you could, and sacrifice all that you are and all that you have to protect them.

In our early years together, neither of us could have predicted the complexities of the medical challenges that Daran would be encountering. However, with God on our sides, and with the absolute best choice in partner, we surrender and have faith that there are always better days ahead.

Key Battle Strategy

To survive the storms of life, the right partner is only one part of the equation. Foundational work on your relationship in the good times with mutual knowledge, respect, and love helps to better prepare you for possible future life complexities.

_____

_____

_____

_____

_____

_____

_____

How rooted in mutual knowledge, respect and love is your relationship? Will it survive battle testing? What are the areas in which you struggle with such as communications, compromise, empathy, support, understanding, trust, and/or love? What three things can you do in the next six months to improve these areas of your relationship to best equip yourselves?

_____

_____

_____

_____

_____

_____

_____

_____

Even though we had been friends for more than three years prior, Daran and I had only been dating about six weeks when this photo was taken. At the time, we were both twenty-eight years old.

Our wedding was a fun, family celebration. Daran and I are joined in this photo by Holly, my sister and maid of honor, and Scotty, Daran's uncle brother and best man.

While it wasn't the wedding we originally envisioned, in hindsight neither of us would change a thing about it. We laugh about how it became our *Big, Fat, Cajun Wedding*!

We finally made it to Greece for our fifteen-year anniversary. It was worth the wait and more. This photo was taken on the top of a cliff in Santorini as our cruise ship is anchored in the distance.

The Battles
— From the Care Coach's Perspective

Armoring Up

As I mentioned in this book's introduction, Ephesians 6:11-18 is my *go-to* Bible passage to armor up for any battles. When I reflect upon it, I envision putting on helmets, breastplates, shields, etc. to prepare hypothetically. However, in real life, my equipment is far less literal and visual yet far more practical and mainstream.

Before I do anything, I pray for God's Hedge of Protection to provide the best armor for the challenge. Through many years and lots of battle testing, my walk has intentionally taken me closer to God, as has my ability to truly listen to His Word for Guidance and Wisdom in the fiery trials.

With God as an integral part of our marriage, an infinite facet of my armor is our love for one another. For Daran and me, it's no coincidence that the words *amore* and *armor* are such similarly spelled words. They are closely intertwined because our love is the power that propels us to work collaboratively with one another.

Another part of my armor is goodhearted, belly tickling laughter; it truly is great medicine. Daran's sense of humor is amazing, and so is his contagious laugh and ability to create elaborate and embellished stories, told using his spot-on impressions and even an emphasized Cajun accent. By the way, if you've ever heard *Boudreaux and Thibodeaux* Cajun jokes, you will search high and low to find anyone who can tell them better than Daran.

After more than two decades together, Daran has even perfected his imitation of my voice by inflating his pitch and inflection. Since I tend to lean more towards being a serious, intense, busybody, his sense of humor lightens my spirit. I do, however, have a dry, self-deprecating wit and can very much laugh at myself!

Daran and I have often been caught laughing during some of our most challenging times. I joke with him that he's held together with duct tape and bubble gum and that the more common illnesses such as a cold or flu can't be bothered with him! Oh no, if he is going to get sick, he is going to go big with a serious illness that is often terminal in other people.

Illness came into Daran's life early. At only six weeks old, he was diagnosed with asthma. He has lived with it, and managed around it his entire life. Asthma, it turns out, was the least serious illness that would strike him. He's prevailed against several life-threatening diseases since then. However, one common denominator in all Daran's health challenges has been his sheer drive and determination to survive.

Daran's Guillain-Barré Battle

In 2002, Daran had a rare allergic reaction to an asthma medication. He ended up in the ICU for five days with a condition called Guillain-Barré Syndrome.

Guillain-Barré Syndrome is a rare disorder in which the body's immune system attacks the nervous system. Basically, it evokes stroke-like symptoms without the lasting side effects that often accompany a stroke.

In Daran, it slowly started with tingling and weakness in his feet and legs. These sensations then began spreading to his pelvis and his upper body and eventually caused slurred speech and a swollen tongue that impaired his breathing. Unabated for several days, he went to the emergency room where he was diagnosed and rushed to the ICU.

Because this disease is so rare, treatment options at the time were limited. There were two treatments to choose from: 1) a new, unproven procedure called plasmapheresis, or 2) a natural process whereby the doctors would allow the patient's body to fall into a full coma, and then slowly reemerge months or years later once the condition had cleared the patient's system. After understanding any side effects and as guided by the advisement of his physician, Daran chose plasmapheresis.

The Mayo Clinic defines plasmapheresis as, "a procedure in which the liquid portion of part of your blood (plasma) is removed and separated from your blood cells. The blood cells are then put back into your body, which manufactures more plasma to make up for what was removed. Plasmapheresis may work by ridding plasma of certain antibodies that contribute to the immune system's attack on the peripheral nerves."

The medical team accomplished plasmapheresis by placing a tube into the femoral artery of Daran's groin. That tube was then connected to a machine that slowly washed his blood and then replaced it in his body. The God Miracle in all of this was there were only four of these machines in all of the United States at this time in 2002. Amazingly, one of those four machines was located in Houston, Texas at the exact hospital where Daran was being treated.

I'm going to stop here and back up slightly. This occurred during a time when people weren't as tethered to communication devices as we are today. It was a Friday and I was in an all-day business meeting. At the time, professional etiquette required us to place our clunky Nextel cell phones in our purses or on the belt clip of our slacks, and not check them again until the business day ended.

When I left my meeting that day, I had no fewer than eight voicemail messages from Daran, each one progressively more concerning. As I began my 45-minute drive to get to him through rush-hour traffic, fear was building. You see, one of the messages referenced his *do not resuscitate* wishes. He basically said, "Don't pull the plug. I'll still be in there."

I thought "Holy cow! How did this escalate so quickly?"

When I finally arrived at the hospital, I found that, although he was in the ICU, he was stable and able to tell me about the doctor's plans. The hospital was strict about ICU hours and didn't allow guests to visit with patients for long periods of time, much less overnight. That meant that I would visit as much as I could, for as long as I could, and then go back to our apartment each night, alone.

I remember that first night like it was yesterday. I arrived home very late and decided to do some research. The stories on the Internet were horrific and frightening. Many spoke about how incapacitated the patient would become and how long their recovery took once they awakened from their coma. After only about ten minutes of research, I shut the laptop and proclaimed, "Well, that's not going to be Daran!"

And surely it wasn't. He was determined and self-motivated to be discharged from the hospital quickly. Blessedly, the plasmapheresis trial worked, and after five days in the ICU, he was released from the hospital. His attending physicians and nurses reported that they had never seen anyone released from the ICU directly to their home. That is Daran Landry in action! To the amazement of his medical teams, he would repeat this pattern in his future recoveries.

Once discharged, Daran excelled in three months of occupational and physical therapy. However, the intensity of the work during those therapies wasn't enough for him. His new routine included proceeding to the gym immediately after therapy for his own designed and challenging workouts. The result was that he advanced through recovery quicker.

Even though we weren't married during this illness, it was a precursor for what was to come in our marriage. Rather than retreating, we both dug deep and pressed in to surpass this challenge. Little did we know that our respective experiences and the lessons we learned through this fight for survival would be the foundation for the upcoming battles that lay ahead the next twenty years.

Key Battle Strategy

I'm all for research, within reason. Information is only power when it can be harnessed for good. You can get stuck in analysis paralysis looking for more, hoping for something else. It is important to do the research to verify the quality and timeliness of the information being offered and to ensure that you have the best medical team available. But you must then step aside and trust that the team is doing everything in their power to help your patient.

_____

_____

_____

_____

_____

Care Coach Question

Where are you getting stuck with information overload? Is it creating a roadblock to stifle the quality of care your patient receives? Are you overwhelmed because of it? Is there a ripple effect such that your patient feels and is affected by it?

_____

_____

_____

_____

_____

Daran's Stage 4 Cancer Battle

The seven years after Daran's Guillain-Barré battle were medically uneventful years for us. I had my bouts with endometriosis, but otherwise we were in great physical shape. In fact, if you'd ask any of our friends or family, they would tell you that we were two of the healthiest thirty-something's that they knew.

In the fall of 2007, Daran went to his doctor for an annual exam. His regular general practitioner (GP) noticed one of the lymph nodes in Daran's neck was slightly enlarged. The GP asked him some questions, but all seemed well.

Fast forward to May 2009 when we were one week out from our annual anniversary trip. Daran developed strep throat and saw another doctor in the GP's practice. That doctor also made a note about the same lymph node and told Daran that he should come back for a follow-up visit once he finished the round of antibiotics and when we had returned from our trip.

A month later, Daran followed up with the new GP who sent him to an ear, nose, and throat (ENT) specialist. The ENT took a fine needle aspiration of the fluids in the lymph node. The ENT told Daran that the diagnosis could be many things including Cat Scratch Fever. Always looking for the humor, we noted the irony — Daran is allergic to cats!

A week later, Daran still wasn't concerned and didn't feel the need for me to accompany him to the appointment at which time he would receive the results. However, on the day of the appointment, the feeling in my gut (what I call a God Whisper) told me that something was wrong.

Since the appointment was later in the morning, I first attended a meeting at a client's office for work. The God Whisper became more of a God Shout in its loudness and intensity as the meeting ended. Upon sharing my concerns with my supervisor, who empathetically concurred, I drove to Daran's appointment. Thankfully, the appointment was nearby, and the traffic lights were on my side.

When I arrived at the ENT's office, the nurse had just called Daran back to take his vitals and settle him into an exam room. Daran was surprised that I was there, but I again explained my gut concerns. He shrugged it off.

The ENT walked into the exam room shortly after I did and asked Daran how he was feeling. Instinctively, Daran touched his neck and said, "I'm great; I really think that it's gone down this week."

The ENT then, rather nonchalantly and with zero empathy or bedside manner, said, "I'm going to cut to the chase. It's cancer. It's Stage Four and called squamous cell carcinoma. I'm going to put a scope down your nose and then send you next door to the hospital for a CT scan." The ENT allowed us no opportunity to ask questions. He quickly spun on his heel and left Daran and me alone in the room to figure out what the heck just happened.

In retrospect later, Daran and I compared notes to recall what happened at that moment. In his usual, lighthearted manner, Daran said that he hadn't braced himself for the doctor's news and that his "butt grew feet" as he slid down the chair after hearing the news. Daran also said that he couldn't look at me because I inhaled the deepest breath that he's ever heard. He laughed remembering that he had wondered how there was any oxygen left in the room.

We sat there trying to let our minds catch up to the verbal bomb that the ENT had dropped until finally, the ENT came back into the room. Intuitively, I reached for a pen and whatever paper I could find. I asked him to spell out exactly the type of cancer that Daran had and he did. The ENT performed the obligatory next test which involved an invasive scope with an extra-long cord that he snaked down Daran's nose. This caused Daran's eyes to water and bulge out of his head. It was like some crazy scene from a sci-fi movie. Whoever heard of such a device? The exam was then over, and we left. It was barely 11:00 a.m., but it felt like the day was spent.

Scheduling the CT scan was next. The ENT said that the cancer had metastasized to his lymph nodes from some other location, so it was classified as Stage Four, the worst level of cancer. This scan was needed to identify the primary source so that they could exterminate it before it spread beyond this area.

Our insurance required more than a day's notice to authorize the approval, so that allowed us time to do some research and let the information sink in. It also provided time to tell Daran's sister, his only sibling, face-to-face. We knew that we would need her support to relay the information to his mom. Daran's dad had died from his own cancer battle only eight years before Daran's diagnosis, which magnified the grief and fear we all felt. While his sister was devastated, she was also a pillar of strength on whom we leaned several times throughout the coming months.

Having only been around for five years in 2009, Facebook was relatively new to the public and novel to us as we had only been users for a year or less. But after we broke the news of Daran's diagnosis to our immediate family, we decided to use Facebook to share the news with our broad network of friends. I remember wanting to post some limited information about his diagnosis to ask for as many prayers as possible. This decision would make all the difference in Daran's recovery.

One such blessing came from someone I had met early in my career when I had volunteered with the Kiwanis Club of Acadiana. Unbeknownst to me, one of my co-volunteers and Facebook friends had moved to a suburb of Houston and had transitioned his career to medical device sales. His target market included oncologists in the Texas Medical Center, and one of his best clients and friends was the lead surgeon managing the head and neck department at The University of Texas MD Anderson Cancer Center. MD Anderson is a world-renowned, research hospital for the advancement of cancer treatment. Patients trek across the globe for treatment there, but we lived only fifteen minutes from the main MD Anderson campus in Houston's medical center.

Daran was diagnosed on a Thursday. By the next Monday, thanks to my friend, I had already spoken with the doctor who would become his primary MD Anderson surgeon. Daran's first appointment was scheduled for the following week. I later learned how miraculous it was to have such an expeditious response, though, at the time, it seemed like an eternity to us.

In the days leading up to that first appointment, we were both anxious not knowing what to expect. As you may have gathered, we are both highly driven, Type-A personalities. As such, we both like to know the program so that we can work the program.

Being in limbo, we tried to maintain our regular routine and do the things we normally would. It was not the same, though, as the news weighed heavily on each of us in different ways. We made love one evening and afterward he acted completely like his regular self. I did my best to seem normal outwardly, but inwardly I was not.

I discreetly left our bedroom, went into a closet, fell to my knees, and quietly wept in the corner. My faith wasn't as strong then as it would become in later years, nor had I developed the spiritual or physical armor that I needed to feel adequately equipped for the uncertain future ahead. I tried to envision what it would be like months down the road if he were to survive, but mainly what would happen if he did not. As I reflect now, I see that it would be the first of three pivotal times in the coming years in which life brought me to my knees before God.

MD Anderson is a phenomenal facility. They have all their medical billing and records interwoven, allowing for seamless invoicing which makes things easier on the caregivers. However, MD Anderson is also a large facility making it cumbersome to navigate parking, locations of scans or blood work, and managing doctor's visits. Fortunately, their staff members are always helpful and willing to direct you to where you need to go. That first day was filled with a series of appointments. It was exhausting, but by the end of the day, we had a plan.

First on the agenda, Daran was to have surgery to locate the primary cancer. It was Stage Four cancer because it had spread from some unknown location to his lymph nodes. To attempt to locate the primary source of the cancer, the doctor would be doing a tonsillectomy followed by several biopsies in Daran's head and neck areas. In the end, they never located that main source of cancer, so the program of treatment they individualized for Daran would blast him with as much radiation and chemotherapy as his body could stand to eradicate the cancer.

I often say now that in one hundred years and beyond, his intensive form of treatment will seem barbaric because of how extremely invasive it was. The medical team basically killed all his cells in that area of his body and then brought them back. However, even with the vast, varied, and lasting side effects that he still manages around to this day, we are forever grateful as we know that without that treatment he wouldn't have survived.

That September, Daran started a six-week program of once a week chemotherapy treatments. Upon completion, he began a seven-week, five days per week program of radiation. It concluded on December 17.

Christmas was quiet that year. We typically travel to Louisiana in the days leading up to Christmas to spend time in celebration with both Daran's family and mine. However, because of his compromised immune system, we chose to stay home and celebrated in our own way.

On Christmas Eve, we played soft Christmas music in our living room, with a fire burning in the fireplace, as I wrote thank you notes disguised as Christmas cards to friends and family who had helped us those past few months. A typical, stress-relieving, and fun pastime of his, Daran enjoyed playing a war game on the computer. I sought something to wake up for and give us a reason to get dressed for on Christmas Day. Churches would be packed, so that wasn't a healthy solution. I learned that Houston's Natural Science Museum would be opening at 10:00 a.m. that morning. We decided to be first in line and beat the crowds.

Daran only had enough energy for about a forty-minute visit, but it worked out perfectly as we were in and out before others arrived. It was an unconventional way for us to spend Christmas Day, but just enough to appease our achievement-driven personalities with an accomplishment to check off for the day.

A few days later, we celebrated Christmas with Daran's mom, his sister, our brother-in-law, and our nieces and nephew at their house in a suburb just west of Houston. It was a quiet day but is one of my favorite memories because we were all together. Each of us stood in faith that the worst of the battle was behind us and that Daran's treatment would be successful.

Throughout January and into early February, Daran was in full *marination* mode as the chemicals went to work attacking the cancer cells in his body. He lost eighty-five pounds during the invasive radiation part of the program and was very sick and emaciated. The inside of his throat was burnt to a crisp and had begun a sloughing off and regenerative process. Swallowing caused him pain, and he vomited nearly every liquid or soft food that he could get down.

We wouldn't see the doctors again until mid-February and I remember being very concerned about my ability to take care of Daran while now *on my own*. I often fought self-defeating thoughts about the poor job I was doing because I was non-medically trained or experienced. However, I surprised myself and didn't harm or kill him. Instead, I charged ahead and fumbled through amazed at the personal growth I was experiencing.

While still early in my armoring but slowly getting the hang of it, I leaned on my instinct for detailed planning. For instance, at the beginning of our trips to MD Anderson, I packed a ton of gadgets to distract me and give me something else to focus my attention upon, including a mobile phone, laptop, and tablet. I'm not one of those *Chatty Cathy* people in physician waiting rooms. I don't group share, even when I'm on vacation. I always joke that when we take our anniversary cruises, Daran becomes the *Mayor of the Ship*, while I use that time to cocoon and feed my introverted self.

Being in those hospital and office lobbies was especially hard because I saw many people in vast and varied stages of challenging and vulnerable situations. I recall one day before his radiation program started, Daran needed to visit the MD Anderson dentist to have a mouth plate created to protect his teeth and jaw. This was necessary because there was a chance that he could get something called *dead bone disease,* which included bone loss in his jaw that might eventually lead to jaw removal and replacement. Yes, that really happens.

We were in an entirely new waiting room area filled with patients suffering from other types of cancer. I happened to glance up a few times and something seemed out of sorts. When we were alone again, I asked Daran if he noticed that there were a couple of patients who had masks on that were flush to their faces. He said that there were more than a couple and that obviously they were comfortable without their prosthetic noses here. Naively, I had never even thought that cancer could take someone's nose before. Sadly, I learned that cancer is a thief that can rob anyone of any type of flesh.

Lobby visits never fully eased for me, but I did evolve to be able to help others and receive guidance through some of the conversations in those settings. Later, when Daran was in the radiation part of the program, the lobby was filled with other patients who were both ahead of and behind him in their treatment regimens. As caregivers, we began to compare notes and share what worked for our patients or what didn't work, including things like motivation, food, and medication.

Healthcare professionals are phenomenal, but unless they've walked in a patient's shoes, they can't fully anticipate what to expect.

Some things can only be shared by patients and their caregivers through their own experiences. For example, cancer patients know that during the times when you're receiving radiation treatments, you shouldn't let your food touch anything metal, including utensils, because it will bring an iron taste to the food. So plastic utensils became an integral part of our lives.

Another huge lesson I learned was to maximize your time with your physicians. While he had several appointments at MD Anderson during the week, he would only see his three main doctors (general surgical oncologist, radiation oncologist, and chemotherapy oncologist) once per week. We spent so much time at MD Anderson, Daran and I joked that the "M" and the "D" in MD Anderson's name stand for *most of the day*.

We discovered patience as we released and accepted a different pace of life. We empathized with the medical teams and understood that they weren't delayed on purpose. They would get behind because they were caring for other patients, many with far greater needs than Daran. We learned to be concise and respectful of a doctor's time by being deliberate and prepared to discuss what symptoms were occurring and what we needed.

Systematic coordination was vital to success. I became diligently organized by utilizing an accordion folder containing a variety of essential information that accompanied us to all Daran's appointments. I tabbed it with sections for future appointments; physician and other contact business cards; billing, insurance, and drug information.

For me, the most vital piece of all was a notepad that served as a journal for the physician notes from each visit. In it, I would document the doctor's findings, advice, and any other pertinent information.

I would also highlight any new symptoms or challenges that Daran encountered during the week leading up to the appointment. I would then request a certain medication proactively with his doctor, knowing the kind of medicine to ask for by comparing notes with the other caregivers in the lobby.

Towards the end of his treatment, Daran was very weak and his thoughts were clouded from both the pain and the medicines. It was incumbent upon me to ensure that he was getting the best, most customized care available. This folder kept everything current and orderly in one location, making it an incredibly valuable resource.

As part of his care, Daran and I made a pact early on that as he would start to feel the full and cumulative effects of his treatments, I would push him through in areas that I knew he was capable of accomplishing. Similarly, I would determine the boundary in situations where he struggled most and would offer assistance. Just as he does with so many things, he challenged himself.

At the time, we lived in a three-story townhouse. As he progressed in his program, it would sometimes take Daran fifteen minutes to transfer from one floor to the next. I offered to move our bed from the third to the first floor, but he said no. He knew the importance of the movement and wanted the exercise, no matter how long it took him.

Our pact also included celebrations of milestones, both during and after his treatments. As the only members of our family who lived in Houston, Daran's sister, brother-in-law, and their kids helped motivate him by joining us for cake and fun to commemorate when he was halfway through chemotherapy. Daran also insisted we keep our routine of watching our nephew's Saturday morning football games. Daran didn't want our nieces and nephew to fear that he wasn't going to survive. He knew that the memory of their *papa*, Daran's dad, and his cancer battle and loss was still fresh in their little memories.

During this time, I learned two major lessons that I still practice every day and that I especially carried with me through Daran's next, and most massive battle. Those are: 1) how to surrender and 2) how to accept help from others.

My ability to surrender didn't come about overnight, but then when it did, it was as obvious as the nose on my face. Long before this time, I had proven myself to my employer, so they understood that my routine needed to change. I kept working the same number of hours but shifted my schedule to allow myself to attend all of Daran's treatments and doctor's appointments.

I'm an early bird by nature, as is Daran, so we welcomed an opportunity to take the 6:30 a.m. radiation time slot. I'd dress for work, drive him to radiation, fight my way back home through Houston rush hour traffic, and settle him there with our pups, who were then in charge of his care and entertainment. Yes, you read that correctly. Our pups were fantastic care companions during this time. They gave him a purpose, unconditional love, and lots of laughter. I'll discuss more benefits of puppy therapy in a later chapter.

With Daran at home resting, I would arrive at the office around 9:00 a.m. and put in a full day of work. It was rinse and repeat most days, except for Wednesdays when I'd spend the bulk of the day with him at doctor's visits, scans, and other medical appointments.

I managed things in my strategic way which included being efficient, perhaps to a fault. I was so effective, for example, that I have amnesia to some of my accomplishments during that time. Months and even years later, I learned about some of the great things that I achieved that I had no recollection of. All of that caring, planning, and implementing took its toll, though. I had never known how truly tired a person could become by maintaining such an intense schedule.

It was during that time that I started asking God for *manna for the day*. To me, this symbolized an assurance of provision and assistance that I learned from one of my pastor's sermons explaining Exodus 16 in the Bible. In this passage, God promised Moses and the traveling Israelites that He would provide food sustenance each day, which would last only for that day. In so doing, He required that they surrender and have faith that more was coming the next day.

That concept spoke to me. So, each day, when the alarm clock would sound, I would say, "God, give me enough Grace to get through today." I would walk through that day in His Grace and then, at the end of that day, thank Him for it. It was a simple prayer because quite honestly, I had no energy or brainpower for a longer or more in-depth one. However, it was immensely effective at seeing me through this challenging season.

The second thing that I learned was how to allow others to help us. That proved to be more difficult than it sounds. As you may have gathered from our story thus far, Daran and I are fiercely independent, pull yourselves up by your bootstraps kind of folks. Through God's Blessings and a lot of hard work, we were building a beautiful life through our successful careers.

As I mentioned previously, in the years leading up to Daran's cancer diagnosis, our vast and varied network of friends became our family in Houston. They truly are Divine Connections, God-Ordained.

During the first six weeks or so post-diagnosis, I had collected a list of email addresses of family and friends who requested that

I keep them informed of his progress. It was the easiest mode of communication for me to do it this way, rather than the onesie, twosie emails and phone calls. This was 2009 and we had graduated from our Nextel walkie talkie-type phones to Blackberries, but the mass distribution and on-demand communication media such as texting didn't exist yet.

Several people offered to help us with a variety of things, but I continued to say, "We appreciate your offer, but we've got this. Please pray for us."

Then I received a message that spoke directly to my heart. It was from Randy's best friend who had survived her own cancer battle a few years earlier. She has known me since I was twelve years old. She has seen my growth from an awkward adolescent to an established adult, and she loves Daran and me as a couple. She told me honestly and kindly that I needed to allow others to help us. She explained how, when our friends and family offer to assist us, that they are offering to help us as much for us as they are for themselves. In essence, it blesses others to bless us.

This beautiful, heartfelt way of expressing care broke my attitude about it wide open. It set the stage for my own ability to serve and be obedient to God by helping others in future ways that I could never imagine. We are indeed blessed to be a blessing.

And I am truly amazed at how creative people can be when you open yourself to them. Someone organized a meal chain for us and there were so many meals delivered. One of our friends sent their yard crew once per month to help with our landscaping needs. Another friend cared for our dogs when our days at MD Anderson were exceedingly long.

Two of my friends came over one Saturday morning in early November to help me decorate our house for the holidays. We unpacked our decorations from storage and spent the day laughing. I would never have decorated on my own; I didn't have the energy for it. It made being home that Christmas so much nicer for the two of us. In 2018, one of those friends died after her own cancer battle. I now have a special memory and always think about her when I decorate for Christmas each year.

An integral component of Daran's health story that I would be remiss in not mentioning is Daran's entire immediate family's cancer history.

Daran's mom fought and survived breast cancer in 1997; she has been cancer-free ever since. Daran's dad was diagnosed with stomach cancer that spread to his liver in early 2001 and he lost his battle later that year at fifty years old.

Daran's sister, who I have described as integral to his cancer survival, was also diagnosed with stomach cancer three years after Daran's battle. She was only thirty-eight years old when she lost her own five-month battle in November 2012. She did not want to leave this Earth and her young children, so she fought fiercely to stay.

The second time that life dropped me to my knees was the afternoon of her death. I was in her bedroom with Daran as he directed her in the final hours to go towards the light and cross over towards Jesus and their dad. I left the room, my knees buckled in front of me towards an armchair which caught me, and I prayed for Jesus to be with us all. It was the worst day of my life.

MD Anderson treated all but Daran's mom. They have retrieved her DNA and compared it to the others. There has not been a direct link found, but they are now in the institution's system to continue researching for future generations within our beautiful family.

Key Battle Strategy

Surrender and allow others to help you. If you are comfortable doing so, compare notes with other patients' support members in lobby areas to learn from them and to share with them. Stretch yourself from caregiver to care coach and advocate.

Also, don't forget to create a system of organizing your patient's medical documentation early on.

_____

_____

_____

_____

_____

_____

_____

_____

Care Coach Question

Are you able to learn from others' experiences to advance your patient? Where can you advance yourself from caregiver to care coach?

Do you have a system in place to capture your patient's detailed medical history, medications, current symptoms, and issues if they can't articulate this information for themselves?

I suggest that you prepare an accordion folder containing a variety of essential information to accompany you to all the doctor's appointments. This folder will keep everything current and orderly in one location, making it an incredibly valuable resource.

- Tab your folder with sections for future appointments; physician and other contact business cards; billing, insurance, and drug information.

- Also, include a notepad that will serve as a journal to document physician notes for each visit. In it, document the doctor's findings, advice, and any other pertinent information. Highlight any new symptoms or challenges that your patient encounters during the week leading up to the appointment so that you can report the facts as they occur versus trying to recall on demand.

_____

_____

_____

_____

_____

_____

_____

_____

I joke about how Daran is like Snow White in that animals and kids are drawn to him. Our pups were excellent, care companions during his cancer battle.

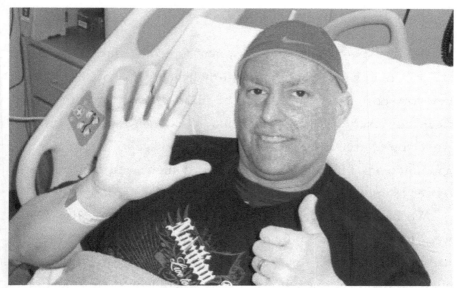

This photo was taken during Daran's sixth and final round of chemotherapy. At this point, the medication's side effects included weight gain, hair loss, and a severe folliculitis infection. He still had a smile on his face, though.

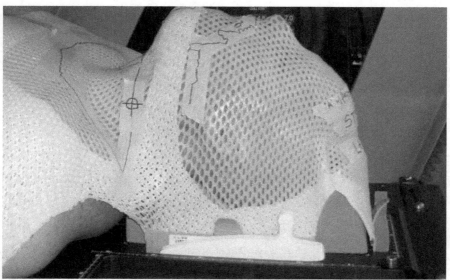

This photo was taken of Daran locked into his radiation mask just before receiving treatment. It was an extreme torture device that he joyfully destroyed upon program completion.

Daran's Ischemic Stroke Battle

Before November 26, 2019, when someone asked how Daran and I were doing, I would respond that there really wasn't anything new to report. We were nearing the mark of Daran's tenth cancer-free anniversary. He had graduated to annual check-ups in MD Anderson's Survivorship Program and was diligent in keeping those appointments. Life was great, we were content, and we considered ourselves immensely blessed.

We began the Tuesday of that week just like any day. Daran went to the gym at 5:00 a.m. for his two-hour workout. We both had several client meetings that day, and we were gearing up for our annual Christmas open house party, scheduled for the upcoming Saturday night. There were nearly one hundred twenty RSVPs from friends who planned to attend, and we were outlining the logistics. Throughout that day, Daran spoke to a few friends and had several conference calls.

Like I typically do, I checked in with him periodically throughout the day. When I contacted him at 3:00 p.m., en route to an early 4:30 p.m. dinner, nothing was amiss. Daran was Daran.

That all changed after his 3:30 p.m. conference call ended. He began exhibiting stroke-like symptoms in our home. As he walked from his office to the kitchen, he was unable to speak and his body became so weak that Randy had to help him to the floor. For context, my uncle, Randy, now lives with us. He recognized what was happening to Daran and called 911. The paramedics were in our house within fifteen minutes.

As soon as the paramedics had Daran under their charge, Randy called me to inform me of the situation and to direct me to the hospital where Daran was being transported. In embarrassing retrospect, I recall that my first naive thought was, "Really, is it that bad to endure the cost of an ambulance?" I had no idea.

As the fourth largest city in the U.S., Houston has several large hospital systems. The paramedics advised taking Daran to Memorial Hermann Hospital, so I left the restaurant to meet them there. Little did I know how pivotal this recommendation would be. Memorial Hermann Hospital is home to the Mischer Neuroscience Institute, one of the top stroke centers in the nation. This is the place that you would choose to treat your brain trauma even if you had all the time in the world to do your research prior to making your decision, which we didn't.

During the drive, I called my sister, Holly, an RN with extensive emergency room experience. Holly's husband is also a tenured RN, so I wanted to ensure that they were aware. More than anything, I needed my sister.

I wasn't sure how I was reacting, I just know that my thoughts were scrambled, so I told her, "Talk to me, not as a sister, but as one of your ER patients. I need to get to the hospital safely and without distractions."

To this day, I don't recall exactly what she said but I do remember how she made me feel. With her calm, reassuring voice, she made me feel loved, safe, and at peace in the eye of the storm. I'm pretty sure we prayed. As I pulled into the ER parking lot, I promised that I would keep her informed.

Somehow, I arrived at the emergency room before the ambulance. In all honesty, I have no memory of how fast I drove. It was nearly 5:00 p.m. by then, two days before Thanksgiving and I was on a stretch of I-10 that was known to back up with traffic. I suppose my car had grown wings!

When the ambulance arrived with Daran, they escorted me back to an ER exam room where a nurse began to brief me. He told me that Daran was unable to speak or move his right arm, leg, or the right side of his face; he couldn't even open his right eye. Daran had been diagnosed with a stroke.

I didn't see Daran immediately. The on-site neurologist wasn't on hand just then, so a doctor at another system facility consulted with me via telemedicine video to walk me through what was happening and advise me of solutions.

As I think on it, I'm amazed and proud of a few things that happened during this time:

1) I had never used any form of telemedicine before. Given the severity of the situation, I am amazed at how quickly my brain adapted to receive the information coming at me in this manner.

2) The neurologist advised me that she was reviewing the CT scan of Daran's brain, in real-time, as we were talking. She said that Daran was one hundred percent paralyzed on his right side and that he was currently experiencing a massive stroke. She complimented Randy for recognizing that something was seriously wrong and acting on it so expeditiously. She indicated that Daran was within the two-hour window necessary to administer a drug called TPA. She advised that TPA has been effective in stopping a stroke in its tracks and has even been shown to reverse some of the side effects. She then asked for my permission to start Daran on a bloodstream infusion of TPA.

Here's where I am proud. Somehow, I had all my faculties, and with a clear mind, I asked her one question, "What is the downside or worst that can happen with TPA?" She said that there is a three percent chance that he could develop a blood clot and die.

I immediately summarized and restated her synopsis to ensure that I understood what she was saying, "So there's a ninety-seven percent chance that TPA will work to stop the stroke?" She affirmed this, so I said, "Go, do it now. I know that my husband wouldn't want to live his life paralyzed if this could save him." I then began signing my life away with numerous documents that quite honestly I didn't have the time to read, nor would I have absorbed anyway.

Still not having seen Daran yet, I made my first phone call to my Landry ally and partner, Scotty. Besides being Daran's uncle brother, confidante, and champion, Scotty is also the executor of our will. He is one of the kindest, most calming people that you will ever meet. He is a great communicator and knows how to deliver even the most challenging messages.

Scotty picked up the phone immediately when I called, which is amazing because as the CEO of a non-profit in the Dallas/Fort Worth area, he is an in-demand, schedule-driven professional. He later told me that he had just arrived home from work and was sitting peacefully under the backyard gazebo as his house was filled with teenagers and college students, home for the Thanksgiving break.

I can hear Scotty's voice in my head now, "Well, hello ma'am!" That was his typical warm way of answering the phone. Directly, I cut to the chase, "Scotty, it's Daran; it's serious; I need you." I was that blunt.

I later learned that, as I was telling him what was happening, he was entering the house to begin throwing whatever he thought he might need into his vehicle. When he called his wife, an executive who at that time was boarding a plane to head home after a week of traveling for work, her first response was, "When are you leaving?" She and I have often said that we cherish how much our husbands love one another. I am forever grateful to her and their family for sharing Scotty with me in the months ahead when he would be *on call* for us.

The biggest ask of Scotty was to call Daran's mom. She would be extremely and justifiably upset. I knew that I didn't have any answers and couldn't speak with her just yet. Additionally, things were chaotic. The medical team needed me to make difficult decisions that could permanently impact Daran's life, so I had to keep calling Scotty back. Somewhere in that time, they rolled Daran into the room with me. He was confused and I tried to reassure him. I explained the highlights of what was happening to him and strongly encouraged him that he would need to fight very hard to get through this.

At that time, I did the only thing that I knew how to do. It was the third instance where life brought me to my knees, but unlike the other times, it was my choice. I squatted in the middle of the floor with my head down and began to pray. One of the nurses thought that I was about to pass out and asked if I needed help. I looked up and told him that I was praying. He then offered to have a chaplain come in, and I took him up on it. I also accepted the chair that he suggested. I had not even noticed it placed in the corner of the small room.

After a few hours that flew by at warp speed in the emergency room, the medical team advised me that a neurosurgeon would be doing an emergency operation to unclog Daran's carotid artery. I then accompanied Daran and the team up the elevator to the ninth floor of the hospital. I remember it clearly because it was now at least 7:30 p.m. and the waiting room was completely empty. I met with the neurosurgeon who told me that the surgery would take about an hour to two hours at the most due to potential complications he foresaw from the likely scar tissue in Daran's neck as a result of the past cancer radiation treatment.

I settled in, knowing that Scotty was on his way and would arrive around midnight. I had notified several friends about Daran's emergency as a call out for prayers. Some offered to come and sit with me at the hospital. In my mind, it was only going to be an hour, so I declined their offers.

I am forever grateful that I have some stubborn friends and that a few of them didn't listen to me. They showed up and found me in that quiet waiting room anyway. I was okay in hour two, but when three hours had passed, the quiet from the unknown was deafening.

What was taking so long? Should I be concerned? I was releasing negative thoughts, fighting to remain optimistic, and praying and pacing the floors as I retreated from my friends and became silent in my mind. I had no updates during the surgery, but nearing the four-hour mark, I stalked the door's tiny window until I finally saw a nurse walking by. I got her attention and asked her to go inside the operating room to inquire for me. Within minutes, I learned that they were wrapping up the surgery and preparing to send Daran to the ICU.

Once out of surgery, the neurosurgeon came out to advise me that he had successfully unclogged the carotid artery in Daran's neck from one hundred percent fully blocked to ninety percent clear. There were other blood vessels in Daran's brain that were opened as well.

The neurosurgeon indicated that it was a good procedure, judging from the post-surgery MRI. However, in no way was Daran out of the woods. We would have to wait because the next forty-eight hours would be the biggest determination of Daran's prognosis for the future.

The neurosurgeon advised me of some worst-case scenarios that I chose to never allow myself to accept. I didn't write them out, nor did I communicate them to anyone. Through God's Healing Hands, the worst of what the doctors predicted never happened. By the way, I still won't tell you what they *prepped* me for because I don't want to give that life. Suffice it to say, I just told myself once again, "Yeah, that's not going to happen to Daran."

By then, it was nearing 1:30 a.m. Scotty had safely arrived at the hospital and our friends left me in his great hands. This hospital allowed both of us to stay with Daran in the ICU. Neither Scotty nor I got any sleep and were there when Daran slowly stirred awake.

Daran was still paralyzed on his entire right side and couldn't open his right eye. He had a feeding tube through his nose and was intubated with a ventilator to assist his breathing. Those post-stroke hours were hard to witness, much less recall, especially once Daran became less sedated and the severity of his new reality settled in on him.

As I've mentioned, Daran knows his body and tests its limits in his workouts each day at the gym. Less than twenty-four hours post-surgery, we noticed that Daran was trying to move his left foot and lower body, but, by appearance, it seemed more like he was restless. Several hours in, we had to reposition him because he was nearly falling out of the bed. We joked that he was trying to make the great escape, but then Scotty realized that Daran was actually trying to move his right foot and leg to try to start rebuilding its abilities. This was even before the rehabilitation team had visited to do their physical and occupational therapy assessments!

The hospital staff removed the breathing tubes the following day. However, we were still unsure if he would be able to swallow. Prior to the stroke, Daran had challenges with choking on food due to the side effects of radiation. His doctors now warned us that this situation would be exacerbated by the stroke. If he didn't pass the *swallow tests* then he would likely be on a feeding tube for the rest of his life.

Well, that didn't happen either. Daran passed the first level of swallow tests that Friday morning and was put on what's called a honey-thick diet. Just as it sounds, everything needed to be made the consistency of honey's thickness to ensure that he didn't choke, aspirate, and then die. Ugh!

Modern medicine has a workaround, though. Did you know that there is a substance that turns liquids, even hot coffee, into a thick sludge? Well, there is, although it did nothing for my Cajun husband's palate. He never complained, though, but focused his energy on the things that he could control.

In what seemed like a short amount of time, he was gaining more and more movement in his lower right half. However, his right arm and hand were completely flaccid for the first five days.

That all changed on Sunday morning at 5:30 a.m. I witnessed Daran use his mind to will his index finger to wiggle. It was the most beautiful and miraculous thing that I have ever seen, a true testament to God's Healing Powers.

At first, it was ever so slightly. By the time his doctor came in later that day, he could squeeze her hand. It brought tears to her eyes. She said that she's never seen anyone get there that fast. Of course, that's Daran.

Not all things began working as easily. While he was able to open his right eye in the first few days, any speech or communication was far more challenging. He couldn't make any sound for the first four days post-stroke.

All in all, I knew that his body would come back physically. It's what Daran's determination has proven that he can make himself do. Speech and communication advancement proved much more difficult.

In total, Daran spent twenty-four days in two of the Memorial Hermann Hospitals and the TIRR Memorial Hermann inpatient treatment facility. He then spent another eight months in the TIRR Memorial Hermann outpatient rehabilitation program for speech, physical, and occupational therapy. He was not only an inspiration to the other patients, but to the healthcare staff and many of his family and friends.

We later learned that if ever there is a part of the brain that you don't want a stroke to affect, it's the area that Daran's stroke impacted. It's that part of the brain where all of the central intelligence is knitted together. In a six-month, post-stroke neurologist visit, his doctor commended Daran on his progress. While there was still much work to do, his neurologist indicated that he couldn't hope to be in a better position.

Daran didn't do it alone. God worked miracles through thousands of prayers, offered worldwide, to restore his health. My prayer over him throughout the day was, "Father, we know that you are Jehovah Rapha, Our Healer. We stand in faith that you have the power to heal Daran from the top of his head to the tips of his toes; and that Daran's cells will be regenerated to their original factory settings as from his mother's womb. We've seen you move mountains on our behalf in the past and know that you will do it again in the future. In Jesus' Name, we pray. Amen."

It is not an exaggeration to say that I have witnessed miracles, because even the experts were amazed by his progress.

Key Battle Strategy

Miracles surround us every day. Don't forget to look for God's Hands at work in everything, and then to thank Him for His Grace, Glory and Favor.

_____

_____

_____

_____

_____

_____

_____

_____

Care Coach Question

Are you trying to jump too far down the road in your thinking and planning, thus trying to anticipate the recovery? Breathe and take in the smallest of accomplishments. Cumulatively, they amass to big victories.

_____

_____

_____

_____

_____

_____

_____

In all the years that I have known Daran, he has never grown his beard out for more than a few days. Because he couldn't shave himself, nor did he want me to try shaving him, we saw what it would look like fully grown out. He's handsome either way, but I still prefer him cleanly shaven.

Battle Differences

In the trenches of the stroke battle, someone asked me, "What was worse, the cancer or the stroke?" Hands down, it has been the stroke.

After his cancer recovery, I often referred to Daran's cancer as a shadow that would follow us. Each new ache, pain, or odd test result could have sent our minds into a downward worry spiral. However, at no time after his cancer battle was Daran ever unable to speak for himself, feed himself, or take care of his personal hygiene and biological needs.

In a matter of minutes following his stroke, my partner and protector became my dependent. The cancer diagnosis and then the treatment program's aftermath evolved over the months and even years to a point where Daran and I became accustomed and then adjusted accordingly to the side effects.

In contrast, the stroke attacked suddenly, without warning or preparation. Its side effects were more dramatic and life-altering, affecting even the tiniest of individual tasks. His booming voice, jovial disposition, contagious laughter, and sense of humor were stripped away. After his stroke, these were among the things I mourned most and longed for so much more.

I also missed his hugs. I've always experienced someone's sincerity by feeling it conveyed through their hugs. It was something that I picked up at an early age from my grandfather who was a *Grade A Hugger*. Like my grandfather, Daran is a phenomenal hugger. He squeezes you just to the point where it hurts in a good, fun way. That was compromised as well because he couldn't make his right-side, including his diaphragm, work fully. (Note: With much hard work and loads of practicing, Daran's barrel squeezes have almost fully returned seven months post-stroke. This took a lot of determination; his hugs were lopsided at first since he had to recover the use of his right upper body and arm. I have not allowed this to go unnoticed and welcome every chance that I can to sneak one in!)

So yes, while cancer is scary, the shadow it casts is smaller than the vast depths of the ominous darkness that come with a stroke.

Each moment that we mark since the day of the stroke is an achievement. The statistics show that the chances for another stroke are twenty-five percent higher within the first days, weeks, months, and the first year of the original stroke date. We are immensely blessed, and we know it.

Key Battle Strategy

Cherish every single day as a gift and try to acknowledge (whether physically or mentally) and communicate at least one achievement that your patient has made.

_____

_____

_____

_____

_____

_____

_____

How can you graciously reflect on a few successes each day as a reminder of hope and as encouragement for your patient? Look for even the smallest of triumphs by documenting in a journal or on a wallboard and calling them out. Your patient will love and welcome it!

_____

_____

_____

_____

_____

_____

_____

~ ℔ ~

Daran is affectionate and forever giving barrel hugs. This was something I deeply missed post-stroke.

This photo is just one of the many photos that we have in our collection of us hugging and smiling. Because it's such a huge way that we demonstrate our love, it was even more deeply missed when Daran could no longer hug for the several months post-stroke.

Strategies as a Care Coach

My Warrior Heart

Warrior, fighter, determined, grit, tenacious, and scrappy. Whatever descriptor you can think of that means *never give up*, that's what defines my husband. I have a front-row seat to experience it in action, but I am not the only one that witnesses it. Anyone that meets him sees it. He has been this way his whole life, no matter the task. He is a warrior, but he is also so much more...

As tough as he is, he equally has a kind soul. Early on in our dating days, he was driving a long distance for work; I believe he was somewhere in Central Texas. We were on the phone, deep in conversation when he abruptly told me that he needed to jump off the call. He called back about five minutes later. I was concerned, but he told me that nothing was wrong. He explained that he had to turn back to help a turtle that was crossing the road to be sure it wouldn't get hit.

This was Daran being Daran and even though he didn't do it to impress me, it did. That small gesture was sweet and considerate. His passion for rescuing and caring for animals is one of the things that we share. It transfers to people as well. That is one of the biggest reasons he's beloved by those who know him.

I don't want you to think that I'm putting him on a pedestal. Daran is in no way perfect. He's been known to have a temper and can be impatient, but never towards me or others. His impatience is pointed toward himself and shows up when he doesn't feel like he is fulfilling his own, very high expectations.

The stroke has changed him, and if anything, he is now an even sweeter, gentler man. His impatience has nearly ceased, and he embraces each day as it comes.

Knowing Your Patient and Their Strengths

Black Friday, the day after Thanksgiving Day, was less than seventy-two hours post-stroke. At 5:30 a.m. that early morning, I was driving back to the hospital. I had slept very little and needed to be energized. So, I put on what I fondly call "80's Mullet Rock." It's not my typical choice in music, but it has always been Daran's.

As the music blared, and I sang off-pitch at the top of my lungs, God spoke a phrase into my heart — *This is not my story.* When I arrived at the hospital, I communicated that phrase to Daran and conveyed that while this had happened to him, it wasn't a situation where he would remain for long. I knew that if I could remind Daran of who he is and Whose he is, a child of the Most High God, then Daran would be encouraged. I also knew that Daran takes great pride in being the guy who beats the odds to overcome any obstacle in a record amount of time.

That phrase became a part of a makeshift anthem that I would infuse into Daran every chance that I could. Observing his ICU room that morning, I noticed that the whiteboard, which the nurses update with their names and numbers for the day, was only partially used. That's when I had an idea to commandeer and utilize the rest of that space.

I knew that Daran would be looking at it all day, every day. So, I wrote out statements to remind him about who he is. I first wrote, "This Is Not My Story!" I also wrote: "Redeemer, Overcomer, Conqueror!" and "Warrior, Fighter, Determined, Tenacious, Grit, Scrappy!"

Later that Friday evening, I returned home and used my printer to produce some of the photos of our lives, our loved ones, and our travels to remind him of what he was working to reclaim — an active, healthy life. I toted these photos, along with some freezer tape to hang them up with (so that I didn't remove any paint from the hospital room walls) and then re-purposed them for each room that he inhabited over the next twenty-four days, including the ICU, his regular hospital rooms, and inpatient rehab rooms. The photos inspired Daran and they also personalized him to his healthcare professionals who enjoyed seeing them brighten his room. The photos allowed them to engage him in conversation about his family and our vacations in a fun way. They also made the stark and depressing hospital rooms, which are often in need of a fresh paint job, much livelier and more colorful.

Additionally, I taped up blank sheets of paper and began recording *Daran's Milestones of the Day* each day. While it was a simple bulleted list, this daily journal served as a visual recording of his progress through his therapy.

Lastly, I printed out and displayed Daran's Top Five Gallup CliftonStrengths®. As I explained in Chapter One, when there is awareness and integration, the results of this assessment can create a common language, empathy, and appreciation of the worth of each person's respective talents.

As a Gallup-Certified CliftonStrengths Coach, I believe in walking my talk. Daran completed the assessment several years ago. We examined his results in combination with mine as a communication tool to deepen our relationship. It was an experiment in curiosity at a then non-eventful time in our marriage and allowed us to delve into our respective motivations and areas of engagement. We saw our commonalities, but also our differences and how they complement one another to make us a great team.

In my work with clients, I witness people doing their best when they apply their strengths to a task. This works universally across the smallest to largest of tasks. When you can "Name, Claim, and Aim" (a Gallup phrase) your talents, and truly double down on them by building them up through intentional use each day, then you can appreciate that they are almost as unique to you as your thumbprint. Only then can they be called strengths. That is the only way that our strengths have an opportunity to develop into our superpowers.

However, like any muscle, if a talent is unused then it weakens and can actually work against you. For instance, each animal knows its exact purpose and value on this Earth. Imagine a world in which we would observe a giraffe attempting to fly or a fish trying to do anything out of water.

Why isn't that so? It's simple. They know their value, they play to their God-Given Talents and stay in their lane.

Living in our strengths zone provides us with an understanding of how God wired each of us differently and how we are motivated and gain passion by certain things versus others. Daran is a prime example of this.

I placed Daran's Top Five Strengths in his room and provided a copy, along with a detailed explanation, to each of his therapists. I encouraged them to adopt tactics to zero in on how he best achieves his goals.

Daran's Strengths at work positively as superpowers include:

1) Focus

2) Context

3) Significance

4) Activator

5) Achiever

With Context as his second strongest strength, Daran looks back to look forward. I captured the milestones of the day so that he could reflect on them often. This provides a line of sight for him to know where he is on his path.

He also has Achiever and Activator which are both the spark and the fuel to get things done. He once told me that the way that these exhibit in him is that he doesn't want to start anything that he knows he can't finish. One of his favorite phrases is, "Giddy-up." If ever there was a one-word summary of Activator, that would be it.

When he combines Activator with Focus, his number one strength, it means that not only is Daran goal-oriented, but he is determined to accomplish those goals no matter what. It is not uncommon for me to sporadically catch Daran at his desk making a list of one, five, or ten-year goals and objectives. He loves tracking his progress to document his successes.

Significance is Daran's third strongest strength. This is his legacy. Daran has a bigger than life personality. He is known for his overly embellished but highly entertaining stories. It doesn't matter if it's our beloved family, great friends, or complete strangers, he draws a captivated audience. I fondly refer to this as, "Storytime with Uncle Daran."

Additionally, Daran is known for overcoming obstacles and is driven by making a positive impact on the lives of others. To tap into this strength, I reminded him that there were thousands of people praying for him each day and that he was important in all our lives. That would always pump his spirit.

I also told him that I was documenting his story each day to communicate his achievements on Facebook and that God was working through Daran to encourage and inspire others. My daily historical recordkeeping seemed odd for some, but it carried forth the journaling activities Daran initiated during his cancer recovery. Let me explain.

Early in his cancer treatment, on his very first day of chemotherapy, Daran asked me to reach into his backpack and grab the camera that he had packed. In full transparency, I wasn't entirely on-board with documenting his journey through photos and my brain automatically went to the worst-case scenario. What would I do with those photos if he didn't survive?

However, Daran knew otherwise. He had a vision of how he wanted to encourage others through his cancer fight by visually recording the process. Later, he would use those photos to coach many others with similar cancers through their recoveries. It motivates him to know that his testimony helps others in their walk through life's fiery trials.

Self-Awareness and Your Strengths

Many of his doctors, nurses, and therapists told me that they have never seen anyone coach a loved one the way I have Daran. A friend asked me what motivated me to do this, and how I knew what to do.

I can't really explain; it is just who I am. I needed to have a purpose, and my approach to motivating Daran allowed me to contribute to his therapy. It wasn't intentional; it was innate. In retrospect, my armor equipped me to use my strengths to motivate Daran by tapping into his strengths (his armor).

Through self-awareness, I know that I lead with my brain through logic rather than through emotions. It is not that I am unemotional; I just tend to plow through the strategy first and reserve the emotional aspect of things for later. This shone brightly through Daran's cancer battle. I stayed on mission and coached him through his treatments, all the way through his cancer-free proclamation. Four months later, we traveled to Hawaii for our annual trip, this time to celebrate our anniversary, as well as Daran's cancer survivorship. As we were on the shuttle from the airport to the hotel, the sea breeze was blowing as "Somewhere Over the Rainbow" by the Hawaiian vocalist, IZ, played in the background.

Suddenly, I began to sob loudly. It was not a cute, dainty cry either. It was one of those ugly, loud, snot cries. The other shuttle guests looked at me, then glared at Daran as if to ask, "What did you do?" Poor guy, he was clueless. The only explanation I could give him was that I guess I had been holding my breath for over ten months and only then was I able to release it.

As I have traversed the care coaching process, it has been extremely valuable to understand my strengths in tandem with Daran's. This has helped me customize a program specific to Daran. It's not that he wouldn't have gotten to this point on his own. It's just that having a planned program helped him stay engaged and keep his spirits high. It also gave me purpose and allowed me to do what I am armored to do.

My Strengths at work positively as superpowers include:

1) Input

2) Competition

3) Significance

4) Ideation

5) Individualization

As it relates to Daran's stroke recovery, I leveraged Input in a variety of forms. I'm hardwired as a collector of information, people, and things to use in being a resource to someone in the future. When I was a child, I was naturally very curious, and my constant questioning drove most adults, especially my mom, nuts. There was no real focus for my topic *du jour* (or of choice) that day. I was just intrigued by the collection of knowledge.

I used to say that I wished my brain was like a computer with a recycle bin. That way, I could delete some of the content that I deemed unnecessary because my need to accumulate is so voracious. However, I'm now glad that it doesn't, because just when I think I won't need to keep some random fact or memory, then low and behold, I find a great use for it.

During Daran's recoveries, I maximized my Input strength to rally our network of friends and family to support us through his therapy by using communication to inform and engage.

With Ideation as my fourth-strongest strength, ideas are like popcorn for me. I took those ideas and combined them with my Individualization (#5) strength to customize a program catered to Daran's strengths. This tactic not only motivated him but supported him, based upon his passions and talents. Additionally, I even individualized how his healthcare teams might fondly remember him.

You may remember my mentioning that we were set to host over one hundred twenty guests in our home the Saturday after Thanksgiving for our Annual Christmas Open House. Because of this, I had been stockpiling, cooking, baking, and preparing a massive amount of Cajun delicacies, including chicken and sausage gumbo, boudin, and other family recipes. Rather than letting them go to waste, I decided to package some pralines, cookies, and other treats up every few days for the nursing staff to thank them for all that they were doing for us. They all loved it. Randy jokingly observed, "That's so Mrs. Maisel of you!"

That is an example of the Significance strength at work. Daran and I both share it as our third strongest strength. Amazingly, we have never butted heads or have been jealous regarding our desire to have others remember us with admiration. Instead, we understand and appreciate one another for it and are proud of our partner's accomplishments. In this, we are mutual admirers.

Finally, Competition is my second strongest strength. It is a strength that, at times, can also serve as a weakness for me. I hate to lose, especially when I know that I am in control of the outcome.

Regarding my care of Daran, this strength manifests in me as the ultimate coach to drive him through. I believe in him and his overcoming spirit.

Like any muscles with engagement, energy, and passion focused upon them, our strengths only become more acutely powerful with time and battle testing. I see my place in this world and understand that I serve in an unconventional yet valuable way.

I embrace my uniqueness and value my talents so that they will become more robust and I can access them more readily. Only then do they become true strengths that work as my superpowers. My desire is not to be the same today as I was yesterday, last week, or last year. That drive empowers me in my faith and walk with God to be a better person, more empathetic, and in servitude to others.

☙ Key Battle Strategy

Together, we are stronger. When we are self-aware and acknowledge and harness one another's strengths as superpowers, we will accomplish anything.

———————————————————————————————

———————————————————————————————

———————————————————————————————

———————————————————————————————

———————————————————————————————

Care Coach Question

Do you recognize and accept each other for the value that you and your patient bring to the process, or are you self-critical and judgmental? Customizing a care coaching program based upon your and your patient's respective strengths, communication, understanding, and encouragement will be vital to your success. (See the Reference and Lagniappe Section for further details.)

_____

_____

_____

_____

_____

_____

_____

_____

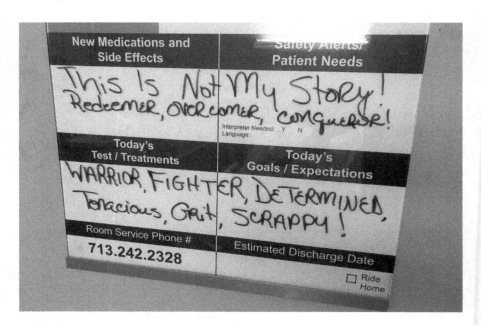

These photos represent the motivational words of encouragement, reminders of his strengths, and collection of photos of our lives that I hung on the walls of his hospital and rehabilitation rooms to inspire Daran post-stroke.

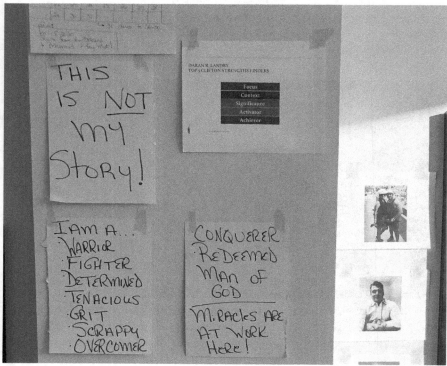

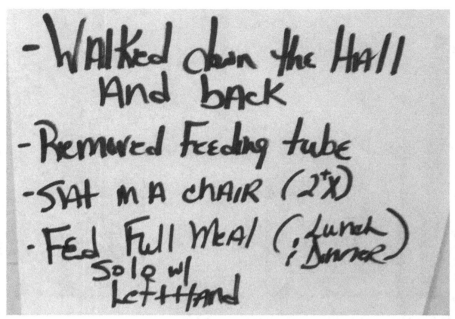

This is an example of one of the daily milestone recordings that I captured to provide context for Daran as a reminder about how far he had progressed day over day, week over week.

From the first chemo treatment, throughout the program, Daran documented his progress as a photo diary. He later used this information to informally counsel and coach others through their similar cancer recoveries.

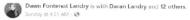
DAY 12: Faith Filled Sunday.

In Matthew 9:29-30, the Bible tells us that '...then Jesus touched their eyes and said, "Let it be done for you according to your faith." And their eyes were opened.'

As you have witnessed these past 11 days, God has worked through your prayers to restore Daran. From the top of his head to the tips of his toes, cells are being regenerated to their original factory settings from his mother's womb. It is not an exaggeration to say that we are witnessing miracles because even the experts are blown away with his progress.

And speaking of progress, here's an update:
- **Daran Landry** regains strength in his right arm each day. Yes; it was only a week ago that he slightly wiggled his right index finger. He can now raise his arm up and engage all fingers.
- As you'll remember, his right leg came back within the first 3 days. He's done much core work to allow him to walk with someone to guide him. Yesterday, he walked without a walker. They're now practicing him on stairs so that he'll be strong to climb up to our bedroom on the second floor of our house.
- He is still on a restricted diet due to the complications of the stroke. Liquids have to be thickened so he doesn't choke. However, he will have a test tomorrow or Tuesday to hopefully graduate to the next level of that diet then (with faith and trust) back to his regular diet eventually.
- He is becoming a little clearer in his speech. Although, in truth, that was the largest and hardest of the impact.

This part is funny and frustrating all at the same time. He gets frustrated because some words just don't come or when they do they only give you part of the phrase. We then just laugh. And laugh.

I played 5,000 and one questions with him yesterday afternoon trying to guess what he was trying to tell me. He makes a sound like I'm a dumb dumb because I don't understand him and we chuckle.

After several hours, I finally figured out what he was trying to tell me. It's the ultimate game of clue. At least we can see the humor in this craziness!

Our faith has worked in combination with your prayers and love to move our God of Healing (Jehovah Rapha). It takes a lot of trust to surrender your life and "hope for the best."

What are you waiting for today? Are you hoping for it in faith? Just as God moved on behalf of Daran and me, we know that He will do the same for you. On this 8th day of the Advent Calendar, what can this large group of followers pray for you?

Daran and I love you so much. Happy Faith Filled Sunday!

PHOTO CAPTION: I couldn't decide on one single photo today, so here's a variety of some of our family photos. He is Poca D to his grandkids and Uncle D to so many. He is beloved for his big, beautiful spirit!

Following Daran's legacy to help others, I knew that it would be important to him to capture his progression. This is an example of one of my daily posts which documented his journey to inform family and friends, and most importantly, request prayers..

Daran and I share a love for travel. This photo was taken during one of our cruises in the Caribbean. By spending such quality time together early, the foundation of our marriage was set so that we can recognize and appreciate one another's superpowers to harness them in challenging times.

CHAPTER
FIVE

Other Key
Battle Strategies

I do not profess to know everything that there is about care coaching. However, the collection of concepts, approaches, and processes that have worked for us during Daran's previous medical challenges are assembled here. I have mentioned some of these in previous chapters of this book.

Care coaching involves the intentional strategy and tactical follow up necessary to be successful while in the trenches. Harnessing my unconventional style, I applied practical, efficient, and effective approaches. That's just how my brain works. I innately ask, "What is the fastest way to get from Point A to Point B with the most productivity?"

Observers of my methods have come to me to garner advice for their own loved ones' battles, and I tell them about the systems that have worked for us in the past. For that reason, and in the hope that these strategies may help you or someone you know, I have captured my ideas, experiences, and lessons learned here. Though this book is not intended to be a manual, this chapter contains action items for your consideration in preparation for life's battles.

❧ Key Battle Strategy

No matter how old you are, you may think "We're too young for this!"

How do I know this? I've had real conversations with spouses of other patients in doctor's offices, hospitals, and physical therapy lobbies. Illness always interrupts plans, no matter if you're still working full-time at a career or you're actively retired. And no one is ever fully ready for those types of life-threatening interruptions, no matter what they tell you or how prepared they think that they are.

_____

_____

_____

_____

❧ Care Coach Question

Have you and your patient discussed your respective last wishes? If not, then do it now, my friend. An illness can pull the rug out from you unexpectedly. What are three things that you are very sure that you don't know about your patient right now? Start with that list; it will grow from there.

_____

_____

_____

_____

Key Battle Strategy

Organized Medical Records

As you have probably concluded from the battle chapter, Daran has an extensive medical history. Those three fights are just the tip of the iceberg in terms of the number of surgeries, procedures, side effects, and medications that he has endured and consumed. Pre-stroke, he managed all the organization and communication of this history on his own. I would regularly attend the really important or annual doctor's appointments with him and chirp in fact or symptom that he might have forgotten. However, I was by no means solely responsible for any of the information.

That all changed the day of the stroke. Suddenly, it was a *big deal* to recall and recite all this life or death information at will and on-demand in front of a variety of healthcare professionals. It's a huge responsibility!

While Daran was in the ICU the second time around, I conceived an idea to develop a human anatomy diagram as a way to denote all the body parts affected by his surgeries and procedures during the past almost fifty years. The graphic would also include notes about all his medications. I planned to laminate it to bring with me to doctor's visits, but I would also have printouts so that I could easily hand them to each receptionist for his medical records. Finally, I would take a picture of it and store it on both of our phones in case of an emergency. I'm happy to say that this graphic is now a reality.

_____

_____

_____

_____

_____

_____

_____

_____

ℰℓ Care Coach Question

Do you have a central repository that contains all your patient's medical history, current conditions, medications, allergies, etc.? If not, then consider creating one now to serve as a guide for the future. If you'd like help to start one, then access my web site for a free download at www.dawnflandry.com.

_____

_____

_____

_____

_____

_____

_____

MEDICAL BACKGROUND

Patient: _____   Date: _____

Medications: Conditions & Procedures:

_____   _____

_____   _____

_____   _____

_____   _____

_____   _____

_____   _____

_____   _____

_____   _____

_____   _____

_____   _____

_____   _____

_____   _____

Additional Notes: _____

_____

                    www.dawnflandry.com

This is the human anatomy diagram that I conceived while Daran was in the ICU for the second time, post-stroke. I use it as a way to denote all the body parts affected by his surgeries and procedures during the past almost fifty years.

✛ 99

Key Battle Strategy

Wills, Medical Powers of Attorney and Financial Accounts

Daran and I have a will, including medical and executor powers of attorney (POA). We did this several years ago because of our untraditional relationship: I don't have any children; he does. Also, we are very close to some of our nieces and nephews and consider a few of them as we would our own children. We needed to have a plan to ensure that our wishes are met in case he passed away before I did, or if we both died together (a possibility since we love to travel so much).

Additionally, because we were well into our careers and somewhat older (we married at thirty-three years old), we chose to keep some of our pre-existing financial accounts separate. This brought challenges post-stroke such as when I needed to pay bills and ensure there was money in the accounts. By the way, just being a spouse is not enough for banks to allow access to accounts if your partner is ill rather than if they have died.

_____

_____

_____

_____

_____

_____

_____

Care Coach Question

Do you have a will and a POA, and are you both listed on all your respective financial, real estate, legal, and other existing accounts? Doing so during a time of mental vitality and physical health will ensure that comprehensive and accurate decisions are made so that they cannot be questioned later. It also ensures that you have immediate access to the financial funds necessary, rather than having to wait for a judgment through probate.

_____

_____

_____

_____

_____

_____

_____

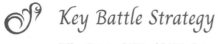
Do you pay attention to the God Whispers? I thought that I did until I didn't.

Consider this a God Shout and not a Whisper — quickly, get your patient/loved one to write down all of their usernames and passwords or show you where those are located.

You see, just two weeks before Daran's stroke, a friend invited me to a financial planning luncheon. I'm not sure why I attended other than I wanted to support my friend who was supporting her friend, the luncheon host. The biggest nugget that I took from that luncheon was that I needed to get Daran to tell me what all his usernames and passwords are. We live in a digital world, don't you know?

My intentions were good, but I got distracted with my business as the year's end approached. I never asked him for the passwords. I mean, really, what pressing reason did I have to at that time? We were completely healthy and showed no signs of the impending battle.

Like I mentioned earlier, Daran was completely incommunicative post-stroke. I couldn't even gain entry into his phone at first. Holly, in her calm, patient, nurse manner, facilitated that access a few days post-stroke, due to her *Mother Earth* way of working with him.

The phone was just one small obstacle. Eventually, I was able to recover all his usernames and passwords. Leveraging our banking, legal, and other connections, I had to execute our POA to gain access to the financial accounts that I wasn't already named on.

Even in a non-stressful medical environment, these actions would have tested my patience. Given this new world of ours, it just complicated the situation.

As a total sidebar, I am often surprised and reminded of the quirky and perplexing characteristics of the English language, especially to non-English speakers. Did you ever notice how patient and patient are spelled the same way? I had never observed that before, but it makes perfect sense. You must have patience when working with a patient.

Do your loved ones a favor and write down all your digital history, along with the account numbers, even if you must secure them in a vault. Or, if you use password manager software, make sure that your loved ones know the master password.

One random day, nearly three months post-stroke, I accidentally learned that Daran had a password keeper app on his phone. By this time, he remembered and was able to tell me the master password to access the app. I jokingly teased him, "You had that all along!" He apologetically replied, "Yes, but I couldn't tell you."

It didn't seem to bother Daran by that later date because he saw me poking with him about it. But it makes me empathize with him, wondering what it would feel like to be stuck in my head with my thoughts unable to express them. I mean really! Can you imagine how horrible it must be to see your loved one struggle with something before your eyes and not be able to articulate the information to help them?

_____

_____

_____

_____

_____

_____

_____

❧ Care Coach Question

Do you have a journal of all usernames and passwords, for yourself and your loved one, or do you use a password keeper app? Don't wait until it's too late like I did. Document it all now. It will save you many headaches in the future.

_____

_____

_____

_____

_____

_____

_____

Key Battle Strategy

Presence Versus Presents

As I mentioned earlier, Daran and I share a love of travel and experiencing different cultures. I've asked him in the past if he would travel as much if he wasn't with me. He said that he might not go to as many exotic places, but he knows that I want to experience those destinations, so he comes along to protect me and carry my suitcases.

The more voyages we take, the more we witness firsthand, visually, and through our conversations, how so many people wait until retirement to do the things that they have always wanted to do. Our philosophy early on was to explore as much as we can now and appreciate our time together instead of waiting until we are too old and frail to fully enjoy it. I am so grateful for all the memories that we have of traveling, exploration, and immersion to so many wonderful countries, especially now when I am uncertain the degree of intensity which Daran will be able to trek around the globe in the future.

∽ Care Coach Question

Tomorrow is never promised. Are you taking advantage of each day's gifts? What are you dreaming of most to do? What are you waiting for?

_____

_____

_____

_____

_____

_____

_____

So much life has happened to us early and I am very appreciative for our vast and varied memories. These photos capture two great examples. The upper photo was taken during our ziplining adventures in Juneau, Alaska. The second photo was taken in St. Thomas, U.S. Virgin Islands at a marine preservation. As you can see, obviously, Daran has much more faith about the sea lion's successful flight than I do!

Life is short. I can only be who I am, love who I can, as I can. If I've learned anything through life's experiences, it's that I choose to live life to the fullest while I am healthy and can enjoy it. I also want to surround myself with people who *get* me, and who I don't feel the need to apologize to for being who I am when I'm around them.

Trust me, I am very self-aware of my flaws. However, I know that there is one thing that I do best and that is to love and fight for my husband. I also know that it would be reciprocated — if the tables were turned, Daran would do the same for me.

During challenging times, it is imperative that you create bumper guards around yourself to serve as a shield from too much advice and intervention. Lots of people have good intentions in wanting to help by sharing their opinions, but it's incumbent upon you to know what works best for you and the person under your care. People pleasing and care coaching rarely work successfully together.

Concurrently, if you are in a supporting role and not the primary care coach, take heed to know when to impose your perspective and when to simply be there providing comfort and moral support.

Do you know the type of cross that you carry? During Daran's stroke recovery, my friends would share their problems with me, then they would catch themselves and say apologetically, "But it's not anywhere near as challenging as your situation." I always believed that to be incorrect.

Pain is pain, no matter the source's depth or type. My pain is no better or worse than your pain, just as how I deal with it is no better or worse than how you would.

After all, this isn't a competition to determine who's in more agony. If it were a competition, it's one that I would graciously step aside for.

The only times that I become challenged with handling my affairs in this manner are:

1) When I become tired and get less filtered because I am an introvert who oftentimes desperately needs a hole to crawl into.

2) When others assume that they know what is best for me and begin making assumptions about how I should do something or be something else.

We should never assume that we know how someone carries their cross and what they should or should not do. We have not walked in their shoes. God has wired each of us differently for a reason. Respect and cherish each person for the value that they bring just as they are.

_____

_____

_____

_____

_____

_____

_____

How do you carry your cross? Can you respect and cherish God's special wiring in both yourself and your patient?

_____

_____

_____

_____

_____

_____

_____

Key Battle Strategy

Not Always Sunshine and Roses

You must prepare yourself in advance because, just as with anything in life, you will hit an unexpected speed bump (or two or five) along the way. When you do, will you throw up your hands and give in, or will you press and stretch deeper into your armoring and trust in God's plan?

That's what I had to do on Day 13 post-stroke. It was a terrible day — a major setback day. While still at the inpatient rehabilitation facility, Daran had a rough night of suffering from abdominal pain. Mid-morning the next day, he started vomiting a massive amount of blood.

Correction, it wasn't just a massive amount of blood. He vomited gobs and gobs of blood that reeked of a smell that I had never encountered before and hope to never experience again. I was paralyzed in fear outside his room as twelve or more medical staff members rushed in to attend to him. I felt so helpless; all I could do was stand outside his room and watch in horror.

He was rushed from that facility to a hospital nearby and remained in the ICU for another five days. That was the scariest afternoon of all time — and he's been through a lot. His blood pressure dropped to 80/45 and remained there for so many hours that I lost count.

Never in any of his prior battles did I seriously contemplate that I might lose him. However, I wasn't so sure that day. What I did know, and repeatedly stated out loud to others and in my head was, "God did not take Daran this far to leave him. Too many people are watching and are inspired by his testimony." And once again, God made it so.

Over the next two and a half days, the medical team pumped five units of blood and three units of platelets into him. He also endured two gastroendoscopy procedures to identify the source, a bleeding ulcer. The team was finally able to stop the bleed and reengage him on Plavix, his anti-stroke medicine. With all that new blood in his system, I knew that the longer he remained off that drug, the more he was susceptible to having another stroke. Fortunately, he stabilized later that week and was discharged back to the inpatient rehab facility.

That's the good news and I could just give you that aspect of it, but there is more to the story. In hindsight, there were about thirty-six hours when I tried to take things into my own hands and control the outcome. He had been transferred to this new hospital and I felt as though his new healthcare professionals weren't providing the same level of care that he had received at the other two facilities in the weeks prior. I also considered having him transferred to the original hospital because of the myriad of new issues that continued to appear.

At one point, it felt as if the medical team would fix one thing, and then that would lead to some other side effect. I half-heartedly quipped that I felt like I was the little Dutch Boy from the childhood Hans Brinker story about the "Dutch Boy and the Dike", trying to plug the next leak, yet having a new one spring up. During that time, I was terrified, exhausted, sad, and had no more words. So, I prayed the only words that I had the energy to pray, "Lord, please!"

I'm not saying that you won't have to step in and loudly vocalize your concerns at times to get the necessary care for your patient. What I am saying is not to lose sight of Who is ultimately in control. Call on Jehovah Rapha, the Lord Our Healer. Once I did, I stood on the statement in faith believing this was a temporary setback in Daran's comeback story. I believed that God had not taken Daran that far, as witnessed by so many, to leave his testimony incomplete!

_____

_____

_____

_____

_____

_____

✐ Care Coach Question

Do you know when it's time to fight and when to let go, fall on your knees and say, "Lord, please!"? Sometimes, it's more about having an awareness that you need to take a break, take a walk or a nap or a bath, eat something, or all of the above. Once you do, the world becomes a different place.

_____

_____

_____

_____

_____

_____

_____

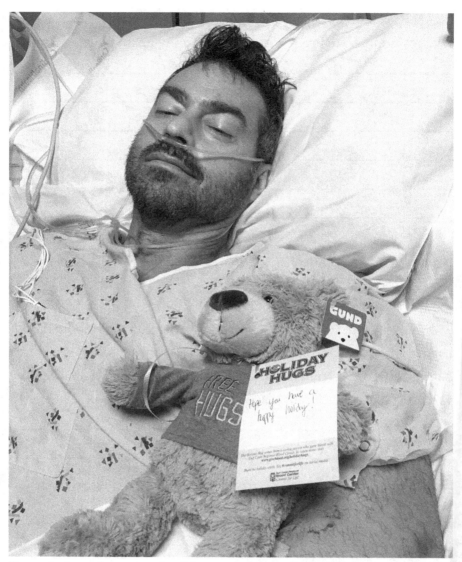

Daran is the only person that I know of that can look this wonderful after so much physically happening to him. This photo was taken in the trenches of his battle when he was receiving new pints of blood and platelets every few hours. Teddy was a gift from the blood bank.

Key Battle Strategy

Coping Mechanisms

Excuse my French. (I'm Cajun French, after all!) This sh-t is hard! The first few days after his unexpected medical events, I was running on adrenaline. I then set a course and got in a tailwind. That's when the endurance test began. It is also when I had to apply the coping mechanisms that I've learned through the years.

One such coping mechanism is that I allowed myself a two-minute pity party. I did what I needed to do. I screamed, I yelled, I cried, etc., for two minutes. Then, I said a prayer and moved on. For me, I knew that wallowing and letting the situation churn in my head wasn't going to change any of it. Most importantly, if Daran wasn't moping, then why should I?

I also intentionally created bumper guards for us where we needed them. That included unplugging digital devices and crawling into our holes when we could, to reset, restore, and be grateful for God's Grace, Glory, and Favor.

What are your coping mechanisms and bumper guards? Outline them ahead of time to ensure that you remember to take time for them in battle periods.

_____

_____

_____

_____

_____

_____

_____

Loneliness is sometimes a byproduct of being a care coach for long durations. No matter how many people are surrounding you, it is normal to still feel isolated in the company of others.

In our situation, so much had changed so quickly. My feelings of seclusion were magnified most when I returned from the hospital each night. Our bed seemed so vast and empty without Daran in it. Even the blow dryer that we share made me sad because it reminded me that he wasn't home.

Enduring all of this during the holidays magnified my feelings. Buildings, stores, houses, roads — when I drove home each night from the hospital, everywhere I looked was decorated for the spirit of the season.

One Saturday evening was especially hard as I envisioned family and friends celebrating as couples, going to parties that Daran and I would typically have attended. I called Holly. She said, "Yeah, but you're not missing anything. We went to one last night and it wasn't any fun."

I told her, "It's not the party that I'm missing. You have a choice; I don't." I had a two-minute pity party that evening. The blessing is that I was refreshed and better in the morning.

I'm sorry to say that the loneliness of being a care coach never fully goes away when you're in the middle of the battle. However, as Daran improved and then finally came home, it became easier to manage.

_____

_____

_____

_____

_____

_____

_____

_____

✑ Care Coach Question

Are you lonely? Do you miss the life that you and your patient once shared? It's okay to mourn that part of your history. However, don't wallow in it for too long, otherwise, you'll become a victim to the circumstances and miss out on the incredible, new experiences that await you — both of you.

_____

_____

_____

_____

_____

_____

_____

Key Battle Strategy

Don't Worry Until It's Time to Worry

Let's face it, despite our best-laid plans, life rarely follows a predictable path. However, I've found that if you relax and breathe through the challenges that you will be pleasantly surprised by the outcome.

Oh, but don't be impressed by this wisdom I'm sharing! I wasn't born with the trait of staying calm in a storm. I come from a long line of worrywarts. I have omitted their names to protect their identities, but they know who they are, and they know that I love them.

You could even call these wonderful people "Worry Warriors." If there is something to worry about, they will find it. If there isn't, they'll conjure something up. They also welcome the company and opportunity to get you worked up right there with them!

Worrying is natural. However, I now choose a different path. I have found that, as soon as I become aware of my worrying, I can opt to go down that road, or I can simply focus on a new, more positive thought. Choosing the positive thought is a healthier option because I know deep down that ninety-nine percent of the things that my overactive imagination concocts never come to fruition. So then, why worry about it?

I learned this mindset by enduring many of Daran's *near misses*. These were instances in which he experienced an odd symptom or received an abnormal test result that could have meant cancer re-occurrence, but it never happened.

Then, in 2016, I was told about Michael Singer's book, *The Surrender Experiment*, and it changed my world. Throughout 2017, I began testing Singer's Surrender Theory. In fact, it felt like because I had declared that I was surrendered and released to whatever presented itself before me, I was challenged even more, and I survived it all.

Living a life surrendered to whatever is put before you that day is the antithesis of the superimposed, strategic planning touted by Corporate America where I work daily. However, I have found that this radical trust is far more fulfilling, and I do accomplish more.

Things will likely not transpire in any manner that I can magnificently create in my head. It will all be better if I take my hands off the wheel. As I mentioned earlier, I adopted this philosophy originally from reflecting on Exodus 16:4 in the Bible in which God promised Moses that He will rain down manna for that day. God gives me provision for each day, one day at a time, and my test is to trust Him.

As I mentioned previously, I have witnessed God's Grace at work in my life. It encourages me to walk through each day. Memorial Stones are measures of my life. They are the times when I can reflect and know that, but for the Grace of God, I would not have made it through that storm. When I profoundly choose to peacefully surrender to God's Will in everything, choosing to quiet my mind and listen to His Still Small Voice, I receive His Guidance and Direction for the future.

There are many days when I get it all wrong and am off course. I know that I am an incredibly imperfect human being. However, I wake up each morning with a sincere heart desiring to try and be better today than I was yesterday, last week, last month, and last year.

_____

_____

_____

_____

_____

_____

♪ Care Coach Question

What are your Memorial Stones or those areas in your life that you know that, but for the Grace of God, you wouldn't have overcome the trials to stand where you are today? Just as He did in the past, know that He will fulfill great things for your future.

_____

_____

_____

_____

_____

_____

_____

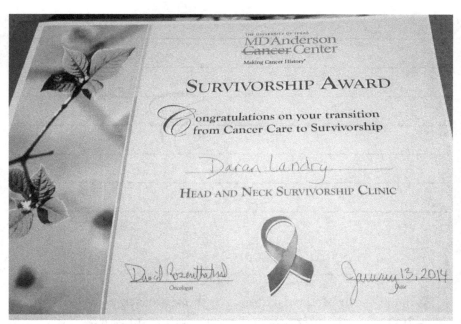

SURVIVORSHIP AWARD

Congratulations on your transition from Cancer Care to Survivorship

Daran Landry

HEAD AND NECK SURVIVORSHIP CLINIC

THE UNIVERSITY OF TEXAS
MD Anderson
Cancer Center
Making Cancer History®

Making it into the cancer survivorship program is a huge deal. It means that you've been cancer-free for five years or more. Even after Daran received this designation, though, cancer follows us like a dark shadow. We made a choice to live life to the fullest rather than to stay in worry or fear.

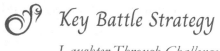
When Daran was in the ICU following the stroke, his arms were so weak that he could not feed himself, even with his non-dominant left hand. Later, we would learn that he had a blood clot in his *good (left) arm* that was causing him pain and immobility.

I began to feed him but did so at the quick pace that I eat. By this time in our marriage, we had developed powerful eye-to-eye communications, so I noticed that he was giving me the *stink eye*. I asked him, "Am I going too fast?" He nodded *yes* enthusiastically.

This gave me an opportunity to counter back, "Hey, remember that I've never had kids, nor have I ever had to feed another human being. How am I to know how to do it correctly?"

I also reminded him that I'm the businesswoman, not the nurse, and maybe he married the wrong sister. If he wanted a nurse, he should have married Holly!

Not only did he and I laugh about it, but Scotty was in the corner snickering as well, trying to be inconspicuous. I asked Scotty if he thought this was funny. Scotty said, "Y'all are cute." I then told Scotty that he had a front-row seat to our marriage. We all laughed!

Laughter was with us through our communication trials in the months that followed as well. Sometimes, certain situations were both humorous and aggravating all at the same time.

In the beginning, Daran would be frustrated because some words just wouldn't come, or when they did, he might only get part of the word out or it would materialize as a new word that he typically would never use. The new words could be really comical and then we would just laugh and laugh.

One Saturday afternoon while he was still in the inpatient rehabilitation center, we were watching a football game on TV. He tried asking me for something, but I couldn't figure out what he was looking for.

Over the next six hours (I kid you not!), I played five thousand and one questions with him trying to guess what he was trying to tell me. At the time, he would make a sound like "Dum, dum, dum." I giggled like I'm a dum-dum because I didn't understand him (something he would never typically say). This made us chuckle.

After several hours, I finally figured out what he was trying to tell me. Somehow, I had to translate that the word "backup" meant that he was asking for his iPhone, which he hadn't asked for in weeks. He wanted me to locate it so that he could play a game on it. I was so thankful to finally have figured it out. It had become the ultimate game of *Password* and I sucked at it. I'm so glad that we could find humor even in that craziness!

It took several months and a lot of hard work, enduring speech therapy three times per week for nearly eight months, but just as the doctors had predicted, Daran's brain began rewiring itself. It has, however, been reconfigured slightly different than it was before.

One fun area of discovery has been Daran's new vocabulary. I never know what new and surprising word he will throw out in a sentence. The new words are always used in the correct context, they're just sometimes unusual to hear coming from him.

For example, we were sitting at our kitchen island having dinner one night. I was reading the newspaper and engrossed in an article, so I was oblivious to what was happening around me. I then heard

Daran say, "The characters are down there." That caught my attention. *Characters, hmm?*

I looked over and all three dogs were surrounding his chair begging him for a treat from his plate. I said, "Yep, they sure are characters!"

These newfound expressions sometimes catch me off guard and cause me to chuckle. Several months post-stroke, I caught myself giggling during one of these instances. I looked over at him to tell him that I wasn't laughing at him but was surprised by the new phrase he used. He said that he knew and that he surprises himself sometimes. We are just so grateful that we can communicate now!

_____

_____

_____

_____

_____

Care Coach Question

Can you lighten your situation by finding humor in even the most challenging of times? Laughter truly is great medicine and is a crucial part of your armoring to make it through the battle attacks.

_____

_____

_____

_____

_____

_____

Daran loves to make people laugh. He plans things ahead of time to surprise us so that he can experience our reactions. It's one of the factors in his life post-stroke that he wants badly to return and is working on diligently. These are photos from years ago of Daran being his funny Daran self.

I cannot overemphasize the importance of having an ally and partner or two (but no more) to serve as a sounding board for decisions. This ally will help you to see around corners and make up for areas in which you aren't experienced, educated, or equipped. I don't advise having any more than two, though. Also, make sure that you define their role(s) in being your ally and partner.

Any more than two and you'll receive too much input. That will confuse you and may lead you to think in circles of indecision. In preparation for their involvement, create a safe space, and give your ally permission to ask you the difficult questions.

It's also vital that your ally know that, while you value their role, you will be the one to make the final decision(s) based upon what's best for you and the patient. Feeling as though you must tiptoe around someone so as not to hurt their feelings will only cloud and delay your decisions. In the long run, your patient will be the one who suffers.

For Daran and me, our decisions about our allies and partners were made clear long before they needed to be. Long ago, Daran and I chose Scotty as the executor of our will. Scotty was selected not only because of his business acumen but also because of his ability to maintain a level head even in the torrent of life's storms.

Scotty is not only crucial to Daran in their mutual love for one another but in knowing that Scotty would be there when I needed him. This was such a comfort to me. During those months, Scotty later told me that he kept a bag packed and in the trunk of his vehicle in case we needed him to head south and make the four-hour drive between Dallas and Houston on a moment's notice.

Scotty also continued his role as the conduit of information back to the larger family. He provided a cushion from constant feedback so that I could keep my focus on Daran.

In a random phone conversation sometime around the eighteenth-day post-stroke, Scotty kindly validated the decisions that I had been making. He told me that, "I've known Daran his whole life. Every decision that you have made is exactly what Daran would have made for himself."

Scotty will never know how much that statement warmed my soul, that day and for many to come. That's what makes him a great ally; he just takes care of things (even me) when we don't even know that we need them.

My other ally is Holly. She is a co-executor of our will, but she and her husband are specifically called out in the medical parts of the document for their vast and varied medical expertise. Both of them have been established, battle-proven RNs for several decades. Their experience became invaluable to us in translating and explaining the medical terminology and providing counsel and direction.

As I shared with them often post-stroke, I know cancer (because I had to learn it through years of on-the-job training with Daran), but I don't know brains.

Well, I had a crash course on brains. Holly was crucial in helping me since she knew what to anticipate and what to ask from the countless number of physicians, nurses, and therapists that were working with Daran.

Holly was also vital because she knows how to handle me. Other than Daran, she's the only one who can. Thankfully, her husband recognized within the first few hours of Daran's stroke that she needed to be here for me. He encouraged her to travel to Houston after they had taken care of childcare logistics at their house.

When Holly arrived, I was still in my business clothes from when I dressed at 5:00 a.m. the morning prior. She allowed me to continue going for a few more hours, then walked up to me and discreetly but emphatically told me that she was taking me home.

By then, I had been up for more than 40 hours without even a small nap. She told me something that only a loving sister could, "You look like a crackhead. You think that you're making sense with what you're saying in your head, but you are only babbling. I don't care if you only take a hot bath and get two hours of sleep. I'm taking you home."

She did what I wouldn't allow anyone else to do. I didn't want to leave Daran and I thought that I was fine. She knew otherwise. I describe to others how she came in to triage me. I will forever be grateful for the love and caring nature of my sister.

℘ Care Coach Question

Who is your ally/partner? Besides being there for decisions, do you have someone that can handle you, the care coach?

_____

_____

_____

_____

_____

_____

_____

Holly and Scotty are two of the most important mainstays in our lives, whether in times of celebration or challenge. These are two examples of their love for us post-stroke. Holly left the sticky note above for me on our bathroom mirror to encourage me. I kept it up throughout Daran's entire twenty-four days away from home and looked to it each morning as a reminder of her love from afar. Scotty is pictured on the following page trying to sleep straight up in the ICU chair, after his all-night vigil with us.

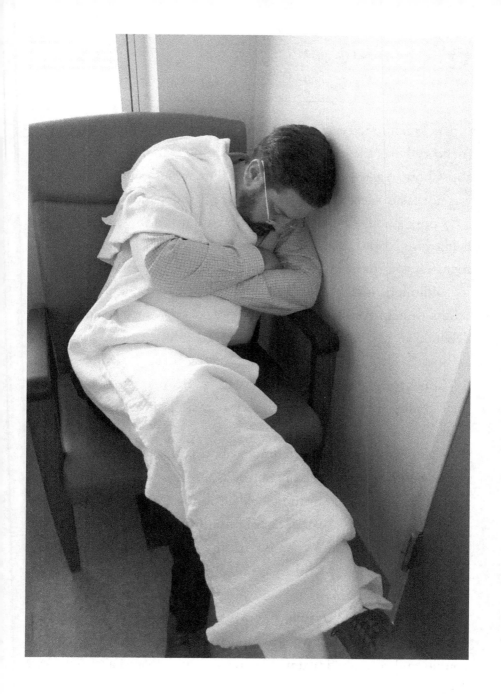

As I mentioned earlier when I relayed the story about Randy's best friend's advice, I learned a *huge* lesson during Daran's cancer program about how to allow others to help you during these times. Trust me, it was not easy to accept. Daran and I are both independent, determined, *get'er* done people. However, when you are down on your knees and living your world's worst nightmare, it takes a village to allow you to focus on your most important priorities — the patient and yourself.

Although, it does take vulnerability to ask for and then allow others to help you. However, God spoke to me once again as I was debating in my head whether to send a call out to our friends for assistance. God told me that He is working through people to bless us. Concurrently, He said that He will favor them exponentially for their kindnesses to us. We are to receive these gifts as a blessing from Him.

I've built a career on communication strategies, so tapping into that experience in my personal life was innate and, in hindsight, was part of me leveraging my individual armoring. As I mentioned, I had an already established email distribution list of nearly four hundred of our closest Houston friends. (It's the one that we use yearly for RSVPs for our annual Christmas party.)

Not only did I need to send the Evite to cancel the party just days before we were to hold it, but I followed up with a mass email correspondence to communicate Daran's emergency and current condition. I combined that with a post to both of our Facebook news feeds.

I then updated Facebook with daily posts each morning at or around 4:00 am. This was when I would routinely wake up and get ready to meet Daran at the hospital or treatment facility each day.

This ritual served three purposes: 1) the posts relayed general information and updates to the masses; 2) they were a way for me to document his testimony so that I would remember all of the nuances of that walk just as Daran had done in his cancer program; and most importantly, 3) they were a therapeutic way for me to write out my feelings as a call for daily prayers.

I always included a pre-stroke photo from the past of Daran in action (solely, with me, or with family members) to remind others that there is always hope and that I have faith that God will deliver him. Thousands around the globe responded with prayers and comments of encouragement.

I sent my email blasts to our Christmas party distribution list less often but provided more detail about Daran's current health conditions and our specific needs. As I learned in Daran's cancer battle, the key to asking for help is to make it specific and even individualize our ask for certain people. By knowing the appropriate timing of our requests and aligning the best tasks to our resources, I garnered participation in the areas that necessitated it the most and had the greatest impact on our present situation.

I always prioritized and asked for *Big Bold Prayers* in my call to our distribution group. However, one thing that I did realize was that I needed to take care of me also. Being at the hospital morning, noon, and night was becoming difficult for me; I was exhausted. When Daran had his second hospitalization in the ICU (which was at Day Thirteen), I again experienced a marathon-long day, this time staying awake for thirty-eight hours. That's when I knew I had to call in reinforcements.

Once out of the ICU, it wasn't that Daran was an invalid; it's just that he couldn't speak for himself and needed someone with him at all times to be his voice. I texted a small group of Daran's closest male friends to rally them and ask if they would commit to one night with him. I called it, "Hanging with Big D!"

Without a second thought, eight of them, varying in age from early thirties to late sixties said, "Yes sign me up!" They would arrive each night at about 7:00 p.m. I would go home to sleep and then get back to the hospital the next morning at 5:30 a.m. to relieve them. It was just enough to help get us over the hump until he was released home.

Additional help came in the form of monetary donations to my Amazon account and checking account through apps like Zelle. Through conservatively budgeting resources, those contributions offset expenses for supplies for our house, food, and dogs for several months following our return home.

I was amazed at how technological innovation had advanced in the ten years between Daran's cancer and stroke battles. Once we returned home, I also requested that a friend help me manage Daran's outpatient rehab appointments through the Lotsa app. That friend had recently acquired his own familiarity with the app in managing his father-in-law's support, so I knew that he was the best person for the task.

Rallying our troops worked seamlessly. Daran sometimes had three days' worth of physical, occupational, and speech therapies per week at the TIRR Memorial Hermann outpatient facility in the first three months post-hospitalization. Our friends would fill up the app's available time slots as soon as our app organizer would post them. We were all astounded with our friends' generosity to shuffle their schedules and give of their own time with Daran as they shuttled him back and forth. And, Daran loved it, too. He welcomed this opportunity to visit with friends who not only delivered news from the outside world but often took him to a restaurant for a meal afterward. It all fed his soul!

Once again, I was surprised at how creative people can be when you open yourself to them. Similar to the cancer battle, the timing of Daran's stroke battle occurred during Christmas. However, our decorations were already up and ready for our party. They stayed up and became background noise, and somewhat of an enigma, for me each night when I arrived home exhausted from the hospital. By the time the holidays were over, I had no energy to pull them down.

Enter Holly and her family. They visited the weekend after New Year's. Like whirling dervishes, Randy, Holly, her husband, my niece, nephew, and I spent two hours tearing down and storing what had taken me three days to put up. It felt like I had decorated a lifetime ago but was only six weeks prior. It was another opportunity to create a Christmas memory that I will forever be thankful for.

It is humbling to be the recipient of such an outpouring of generosity. I've always known that we are loved and that Daran is beloved by family and friends. However, I am overwhelmed by the many people that he has touched. His spirit and his life are a testimony that continues to inspire others (present company included).

One final comment regarding this topic. It was important for me to document each contribution during Daran's battles, but especially post-stroke. Our friends and family did not expect thank you notes from us; that is not why they contributed. However, I wanted to honor each of them with an individual note. As I did, I would say a prayer of gratitude to God for them and ask for God's Hedge of Protection over them. As I mentioned before, they held us up when we couldn't do so ourselves. There is no way that they will ever know how much they mean to us. My heart overflows when I think of them.

_____

_____

_____

_____

_____

℘ Care Coach Question

How can you allow others to help you with tasks for which you don't have the time or energy, but that might enable them to be God's blessing to you? Can you customize your *ask* to certain groups from your friends and family and prioritize your areas of most need?

_____

_____

_____

_____

_____

Day 18: It Takes A Village.

It is humbling to be the recipient of such an outpouring of generosity by you, our family and friends, these past several weeks. We are forever grateful for your prayers (we deem highest on the list), your monetary donations, your concern for my health and the delivery of food to keep me going, your advice/counsel and the errands, etc.

At first, it was not easy to accept. Daran Landry and I are both independent, determined, "get 'er" done people. However, God spoke to me as I was debating this in my head. He said that He is working through people to gift us. Concurrently, He said that He will favor those gifters exponentially for their kindness to us. We are to receive these gifts as a blessing from Him. You are beautiful and we appreciate you. You will never know how important your part of this journey is to us.

Here's a great example of friends coming to the rescue:
After the HUGE speed bump of last week, Daran was approved by insurance to move back to rehab late yesterday pm. (I had called earlier to put some pressure.) They said approval wasn't likely to happen until Monday so this is excellent news!

The challenge was that I forgot his clothes at home. All he had was the gown on his back; I joked that he was like Tarzan! (We live ~45 min/one-way in 5:00 Friday traffic away.).

A friend ran to our home to get the box that another friend packed up for me from rehab earlier this week when we left in the ambulance bc of the emergency bleeding. It is taking a village; so glad that y'all are a part of ours! May God Bless and Keep You, now and always...

Much love,
D&D

PS - I continue to be reminded how bad I am at things such as this! It showed up earlier this week when his arms were weak and he couldn't feed himself. I was feeding him at my pace. We now have an even more powerful eye to eye communication and he gave me the stink eye; I reminded him that I've never had kids nor had to feed another human being. How was I to know how to do it correctly???

At least we can laugh about it. Lord, the stories he will tell when he can articulate his thoughts again!!!

I have always been naturally drawn to the written form of communication. Documenting Daran's status and rallying a call for prayers and assistance in the areas we needed it most was easier for me than I know it might be for many. This is an example of one of the messages that I relayed to our supporters.

Key Battle Strategy

There's No Place Like Home

When we heard that Daran was going to be released to come home, I could not get Dorothy, her red, ruby slippers, and that saying, "There's no place like home!" out of my head.

By then it was December 20, and Daran had spent twenty-four days in the hospitals and inpatient rehabilitation center. There is something to just being quiet and still, surrounded by the people, furry, four-legged souls, and things that you love, in a place where you are most comfortable. When my two hundred fifteen pound Christmas gift was discharged, it was the greatest present that I have ever received.

Once again, my lack of medical expertise made me cautious about taking Daran home. I was especially apprehensive about the volume of medications and technically explicit instructions for administering them throughout the day. That's when I leaned on my extreme organizational skills to develop a process and serve as a guide for following those directions.

Additionally, before we even arrived home, I made an appointment with Daran's general practitioner (GP) for that following week. His GP would serve as an oracle for the development of a strategy to schedule and sequence the numerous follow-up appointments that were now necessary.

Once we arrived, I made phone calls, texts, and emails to allow our loved ones to know that we were home safely. I also was clear about our need to disconnect. I untethered myself from technological devices for more than four days. We set up camp in our bedroom, watched movies, and hung out in our bed with our furry little girls.

I didn't realize how exhausted I was. Little did I know, that was just the beginning of my recovery from the impact.

Although Christmas was within a few days, our holiday celebration was quiet by our choosing. As I learned and fully experienced in the months to come, loud noises and large groups are overwhelming for Daran. Whereas he was once the life of the party with his booming voice and animated stories, he is much quieter now and prefers one-on-one conversations.

A stroke truly is a brain injury. His ability to concentrate on conversations is challenged even in peaceful surroundings; anything otherwise is too taxing on him and requires too much energy.

_____

_____

_____

_____

_____

_____

_____

_____

❧ Care Coach Question

What does your *hobbit hole* look like? Will you take time to untether yourself from electronic gadgets to be still and quiet to allow yourself to rest and reset?

_____

_____

_____

_____

_____

_____

_____

There really is no place like home. It's extra special when you can share it with your furry kids. In these photos, you will see that our new pup was quite pleased to have her daddy home again. She continues to be his sidekick as she grows into a funny firecracker who keeps us laughing.

Once I was able to take a breath and process the prior month's impact, I equated it to being in a time vault where lives around us continued at their regular pace, but we were in our own time zone.

Without knowing it, I was still very much in a fog a month later into January. I tried to return to my normal pace of work, but it felt like I was trying to think through mud. I had never experienced anything like it. Even the smallest of tasks took me five hundred times longer to accomplish. I was highly inefficient and unproductive, and my creative vessel was completely depleted.

During this time, my overachieving and impatient mind would try to command me to accomplish more. In the past, I've referred to that voice as the Drill Sergeant. She is quite annoying. She's a bully and is extremely demanding and judgmental.

After about three weeks of this, I felt as though I was falling into a depression. I didn't want to get out of bed, work, or do anything for that matter. Thankfully, my sisterhood saved me.

I've been a member of a Bible Study of professional women through the organization, 4word, for more than twelve years. Through that time, many of us have walked alongside one another, celebrating the highest of highs and supporting the lowest of lows in our respective lives.

We normally only meet in person each Wednesday at 7:30 a.m. No one ever calls in. That week, I could not make myself get dressed, but I did have the wherewithal to ask to call in. When I did, I broke down in a safe space. They prayed over and for me. That was the turning point.

I reminded myself the next morning when the alarm clock went off to ask God, "Who can I serve today?"

Additionally, up until that point, I was so exhausted that I had no self-awareness about the Drill Sergeant's verbal abuse in my head. Once I did, I realized that I would never talk to a beloved friend the way that I was talking to myself in my head, and if I did try to talk to a friend this way, they wouldn't be my friend anymore.

From then on, when I caught the Drill Sergeant commanding or demanding, I pretended to flick her off my shoulder. This allowed for and opened the space and grace that was needed to heal fully and completely.

Wikipedia defines grace as "forgiveness, repentance, regeneration, and salvation... An accurate, common definition describes grace as the unmerited favor of God toward man."

I believe that grace isn't only by God, but by us to ourselves. I can be very hard on myself, and it's not always easy to grant myself grace. I'm far more apt to advise and grant grace to others than to myself. However, we must find a way to offer it to ourselves, especially in nightmare situations that sometimes become our lives.

_____

_____

_____

_____

_____

_____

Where are you too hard on yourself and are berating yourself with your inner dialogue? Catch yourself midstream and readjust as often as you can. Be kinder to yourself; you're the only you that you have!

_____

_____

_____

_____

_____

_____

_____

Daran and I have always supported one another in our career achievements. The month prior to Daran's stroke, I was honored by the Regional Hispanic Contractors Association (RHCA) with the *Luna Outstanding Executive of the Year Award* as a Senior Executive in the architecture, engineering, or construction industry in Houston. This photo was taken at that event's awards ceremony.

Throughout the first several post-stroke months, I wanted to write down my experiences to share and motivate others and myself. Typically, writing is a therapeutic outlet for me.

However, as I mentioned previously, my thinking vessel was completely drained and dry from exhaustion. I had nothing creative to offer and there were many self-critical thoughts playing in my head. In the first several months post-discharge, when I did have a client deadline, it took all of my power to muster up the energy to be present and deliver.

With some self-awareness about it, here's what I did (and continue to do) to begin to dig myself out:

1) I allow myself the time needed to heal by giving myself the grace that I so desperately need. This has been the most challenging for me. I'm a Type A+++ personality. I get stuff done! Operating at a slower pace isn't typically in my DNA. However, I have had to learn to speak kinder to myself.

2) I catch myself when I'm stuck in worry or doubt about the future. Just as I did in 2017 in my *Surrender Year*, I embrace whatever is in the path before me, living for the *manna* of the day. This recent battle reinforced my need to allow life to flow and then take advantage of the path that lies ahead.

3) I look for, and live in, appreciation for even the smallest of victories. When, in the foundation of your being, you live with an attitude of gratitude rather than lack, then you exude and attract peace and contentment.

Slowly, my mojo began to reveal herself, initially through my self-healing and then in opportunities to serve my clients, family, and friends.

I realized the importance of embracing those occurrences and accepting that it would take time before I became fully restored. When I did, it returned in waves and now feels like a welcome home.

Additionally, the timing of the COVID-19 pandemic was a gift of time that I never would have given myself. I am sensitive to the many lives lost, as well as economic hardship, from the coronavirus. Personally, it had severe and deep ramifications on my business as well. That's not what I'm speaking of.

What I am referencing is that during the months of stay at home ordinances and self-quarantining, I was able to give myself the space that I needed to mourn our former lives and heal from all that we had endured during those first few months post-stroke. I had no idea how much I needed it, but I took full advantage of it.

It was during this time that I started and completed this book. While cathartic, writing this memoir also revealed and caused the eruption of many emotions that I had suppressed and needed to discharge. My restoration continues…

_____

_____

_____

_____

_____

_____

_____

_____

♪ Care Coach Question

Where are you stuck? Through quiet introspection, can you dig deep to identify any areas needing restoration, healing, forgiveness, or mourning that may be holding you back from your own emotional and mental health recovery?

_____

_____

_____

_____

_____

_____

_____

The physicality of being a care coach takes its toll. Despite my best intentions, eating was the one thing that I kept forgetting to do. I dropped fifteen pounds overnight just because I would lose track of time in the vortex of those hospital walls. Concerned for my well-being, many friends brought food to me and that helped.

However, only I can take care of the emotional and mental aspect of my care coaching role. I learned that especially after Daran's cancer battle.

I'm going to say something here that may sound selfish, but it needs to be acknowledged and considered if you are to be a care coach, caregiver, carer, or whatever you call yourself. You can't lose yourself.

You see, I lost myself when Daran fought cancer. For over a year following that battle, I felt as though I was the lady whose husband had cancer. In kindness, it was the first thing that people would ask me about after their initial greeting.

At that time, I struggled to recover my identity because it was so interwoven with Daran's. I loved being his care coach. I cherished all the time that I spent with him. I wouldn't change a thing about that aspect of it. However, I hadn't kept anything for myself.

After the initial shock and endorphin rush from Daran's stroke battle, I remembered to carve out time for myself. As I continue to care for Daran, I make time to spend with friends. I especially prioritize my time with God privately and in my 4word Bible Study. My Sisters in Christ will never know how much they helped me, nor how grateful I am to them.

_____

_____

_____

_____

_____

_____

_____

_____

ℰ *Care Coach Question*

What's the piece that's reserved only for you? Can you carve it out and set it aside for your well-being?

_____

_____

_____

_____

_____

_____

_____

_____

While I am nowhere near as comical as Daran is, with his influence through the years, I don't take myself as seriously as I used to. This photo shows my lighthearted side.

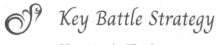
Prior to Daran's cancer battle, I had never felt the overwhelming *power of prayers*.

When family or friends would say, "I'm praying for you," I'd smile and thank them for those prayers, but in the back of my mind, I'd wonder about the prayer's impact or ability to work.

That all changed for me when Daran walked through cancer, and then resoundingly through his stroke battle. There are no words to describe it, but you can feel the mass cumulative power of people praying for you. I absolutely believe that God works miracles through those prayers because I have seen it beautifully demonstrated with my own eyes.

Here's another miracle that I deeply know could only come from the Hands of God. As is the case when you have any medical procedures, but especially a major medical event, you dread when all the provider invoices start to roll in. That's only human. However, just as I did with Daran's health, I released control of the outcome to God. I told Him that no matter what, I knew that He would provide a way out of it financially as well.

Things were eerily quiet the month of January, but our insurance broker (who is amazing, by the way) told me that this was common. End of year medical invoices can sometimes take two or three months to arrive. With still no word in early February, she offered to visit our house and jointly call Blue Cross Blue Shield with me. Who does that?

We were fortunate in that we were assisted by a kind and thorough insurance customer representative who patiently researched each claim and answered all our questions. In the end, she happily delivered the message that, since Daran had already met his deductible for the year, all twenty-four days of his hospitalization were covered stating, "the patient has no fiscal responsibility."

With a total of thirteen days in the hospital (eleven of which were in the ICU) and eleven days in inpatient rehab, the cumulative bill was nearly $500,000. Our insurance broker told me that she's never seen anything like it in her twenty-six-year career. I was amazed and thanked God that He did it again. His testimony in our lives is extraordinary!

You know, I have often wondered how people with little to no faith get through battles such as we've endured. There is no way that I would still be standing unless I had a relationship with God through Jesus Christ and the Holy Spirit and knew that they were walking before us, guiding our steps.

I know that it takes a lot of trust to surrender and *hope for the best*, but I have seen how doing so makes day-to-day life worth living.

_____

_____

_____

_____

_____

_____

_____

_____

Where are the areas in your life that you haven't fully surrendered to serve? Can you release them, knowing that God has you in the Palms of His Hands?

_____

_____

_____

_____

_____

_____

_____

~ ♭ ~

But by the Grace of God, Daran has survived. We know that God has a great purpose for Daran's life. This photo was taken just weeks after the completion of his cancer treatments. It's indicative of where and to Whom we look first as we head into battle.

CHAPTER
SIX

Reminding the Patient Who They Are

Key Battle Strategy

Reality Sets In

I haven't known Daran the longest, but I know him best. I know how to motivate him, and I know how to aggravate him, unintentionally of course.

Early on post-stroke, there was a span of about thirty-six hours when Daran couldn't move his right side and he shed tears during most of his waking hours. At one point, I got in bed with him so that I could look eyeball-to-eyeball at him. I asked him if he was sad. He nodded yes. I asked him if he was feeling sorry for himself. He again nodded yes. I told him that of everyone I know, he had every right to feel sorry for himself. His present situation sucked and it would be a long road to get back, but I told him that I knew if anyone could do it, he could.

I also reassured him that I was not going anywhere and that he couldn't get rid of me that easily!

From years before when he was about halfway through his cancer radiation treatments, I distinctly remember a passing comment that Daran's oncologist's nurse, made to us during one of his appointments. The nurse walked in to take Daran's vitals and get his weekly update.

When he saw me, he joked, "Oh, you're still here." I replied, "Of course, I'm still here. Where else would I be?" The nurse then commented, "Well, at about this juncture in the treatment program, some patients see their spouses or significant others disappear. Those overwhelmed family members say, 'I didn't sign up for this.'"

I was dumbfounded with that notion; it seemed so foreign to me. Although, I know that if you aren't armored for these tough life challenges, they will test the strongest of people and shake the foundation of relationships.

_____

_____

_____

_____

_____

_____

_____

_____

⟡ *Care Coach Question*

Does your patient know that you're in it with them for the long haul? Have you vocalized it? Don't assume; they need to hear you say it. And say it often!

_____

_____

_____

_____

In this photo, others struggled to see Daran. However, my sight never wavered. I didn't see how truly different he looked or the impact that the cancer treatments had on him physically until I saw this photo months later. God protects us even when we don't realize it.

Key Battle Strategy

Slow and Strategic Visits

Daran's spirits slowly began to lift as each day passed. In the early days, post-stroke, his friends were calling and requesting to visit him, but he did not want to see any outside guests. He was still processing everything and did not want sympathy.

He finally agreed to allow a visitor here and there. I respected his integrity throughout. It was something that I insisted upon. During the first month, we agreed that the only non-family visitors would be our male friends. There were a lot of medical devices and rehab activities happening, not to mention the revealing hospital gowns. Daran has always prided himself on his appearance and I wanted to preserve his dignity.

No matter how much I tried to prepare guests in advance of their visit with him, they were still taken aback about how much the stroke had impaired him, especially in the first few weeks. Because he couldn't speak even a word early on, some visitors were uncomfortable with the silence or overall situation so they would talk at him, while others would speak to him as though he was a four-year-old child rather than the intelligent, adult man that he has always been. Still, others comfortably sat with him and allowed him the time and space that he needed to connect his thoughts to articulated words.

Watching Daran with visitors who patiently waited for him to speak was beautiful to experience. He became more relaxed, talkative, expressive, and confident, and then grew to even be humorous.

It makes perfect sense, right? Have you ever been in a conversation with someone who impatiently tries to finish your sentences for you, but gets it all wrong? I don't know about you, but I leave those conversations feeling anything but listened to, heard, or understood.

One impactful takeaway from this experience for me is that by throttling back the urge to speak in the silence, exercising more patience, and allowing more space in the conversations, I have witnessed that it always brings a harvest of the greatest results. I see this insight as applicable in all aspects of my life now.

_____

_____

_____

_____

_____

Care Coach Question

Who brings out the best in your patient? Which guests are challenges for them? Is there a way to shield your patient against them or at least schedule those visitors in shorter intervals?

_____

_____

_____

_____

_____

Fundamental to reminding Daran of who he is, it was especially important to focus on the things that I know he loves. That's why when we checked in to the inpatient rehab and were waiting for someone to come and greet us, rather than sitting there being reactive, I decided to proactively take a walk (wheeling him in his wheelchair) to visit the facility's gym. I knew that by seeing the gym Daran would be motivated by looking forward to his workouts. While others would later refer to it as the torture chamber, Daran always welcomed an opportunity to push himself in the physical part of his recovery.

As I mentioned previously, Daran and I are passionate animal advocates. Our furry, four-legged kids were a vital part of his cancer recovery. I refer to those three pups as the "originals"; all were rescues who lived well into their senior years. While all of those pups have crossed over the rainbow bridge, our two new rescued girls played a pivotal role as makeshift therapy dogs in his recovery in the months post-stroke.

We have witnessed that it doesn't matter if it's an adult dog, or a developmentally disabled one, or even a puppy, the way that our dogs have engaged with Daran through both his cancer and his post-stroke battles has taught us something. They respond to him as though they know he's ill with the extra tenderness and attentiveness that they show him. Caring for them gives Daran a purpose and is bonus therapy for him. Also, our pups don't judge him or try to correct him. They are enamored with Daran for the loving, treat dispenser that he is!

Care Coach Question

Can you double down on the things your patient loves most? A joyful purpose feeds the spirit.

Can you just see the puppy love that she has for Daran? Yes, this pup is a master manipulator, but she's also excellent therapy for him. As an added bonus, she's extra cute and cuddly!

Key Battle Strategy

Treating Him as the Man He Still Is

I never forgot that my husband was in there, so I've never considered him any other way, even in the early days post-stroke. You see, he was always in there and knew what he wanted to say. It's just that the wires didn't connect well between his brain and his mouth or his hands to allow him to freely speak or write.

I have made sure to preserve his manhood by never treating him like a child. He didn't want special treatment during his cancer program, and I knew that he wouldn't wish to be treated like a forty-eight-year-old invalid post-stroke. I was certain that I could help him in a way that was encouraging and empowering. But, I would do it in a way that would allow him to grow his abilities back.

Even though he asked that I speak for him, especially on technical and complicated medical matters, I never assumed that I knew what he wanted. As time passed, we developed a shorthand way of communicating through facial expressions and glances. This was fairly easy because it was based on twenty-four years of friendship.

Did I always get it right? No, but I tried very hard. Through self-reflection, I found that I was the most ineffective when I was rushed, distracted, or tired.

I was always truthful with him, even when the information I had to share was scary. I assembled the research and then got his opinion and buy-in on all decisions. While he always agreed with me, I still wanted him to have a voice. It didn't matter what the decision was about, and that included those dealing with treatment facilities and finances, for example. I did it in a way that didn't burden him but instead made him feel included in the process.

I also always honored his wishes, which was not always easy. For instance, I did not take offense or take it personally when, from the beginning, he didn't want me to be a part of his speech therapy. I knew that it was hard for him to do it in front of me. In some ways, I can see that it could be emasculating. He needed to keep that for himself. His speech pathologists commended me for stepping aside and found ways to keep me informed of his progress. They would involve me when appropriate, for specific decisions and updates.

Planning for his return home from the inpatient rehabilitation center was challenging. While I made the necessary accommodations for medical equipment, there was more to consider, but never did I naively anticipate having to address an issue that infringed upon his civil liberties. Through the years, Daran had amassed a gun and ammunition collection, not for hunting but as a range sport shooting hobby.

Stepping up as my ally to proactively counsel me, Holly pointed out how Daran might develop depression. She advised me to consider securing his guns by changing the gun safe code or even removing them from our house for a time.

I was stunned: 1) because the thought never crossed my mind, and 2) because I know first-hand the aftermath of suicide. You see, my paternal grandfather committed suicide by gun when I was ten years old. My paternal grandmother was the one who found him. This sent shock waves of devastation through that side of my family, especially for my dad, as his manic actions towards us worsened following his father's death.

Remembering all those feelings from my childhood, Holly's advice stopped me in my tracks and simultaneously sucker-punched me to the core. So, I dealt with it much as I deal with everything; I prayed about it for a few days. I then used my armoring to drive my decision-making and strategy.

While I spoke to Scotty about it, ultimately, the handling of the situation would be in my court. I also prepped one of Daran's friends who he shoots with regarding the situation and asked him if he'd store Daran's guns if we chose to go in that direction. Finally, I talked to Daran's doctor to garner professional counsel about it.

I then strategically planned out my conversation to address the subject with Daran in a manner that was respectful of him and preserved the foundation of our relationship. I chose an appropriate time and had a directly pointed discussion with him. I told him of my concern. Even with his limited speaking ability at that time, his initial facial reaction was quite revealing. It was one of disgust like that thought would never have come into his mind. And while he couldn't verbally communicate his reasons for living, I knew what he was saying when he started listing many of his loved ones even when he couldn't find the names of some of them individually.

Leaning on his word as his bond once again, I bent over really close to him and said, "Daran Ray Landry, you better not let me find you that way." Daran made a promise that I wouldn't, and I trust him. Besides his own reasons for living, he knows the story about my grandfather and the impact that it had on me and my family.

I don't advise taking this path unless you truly have a trusting bond with your patient. I know that depression is an illness, and I am on the lookout for any changes in Daran. I just knew at that time that I needed to respect the integrity of our marriage and Daran as a man. Otherwise, what's the point?

_____

_____

_____

_____

_____

_____

_____

♫ Care Coach Question

What are some of the areas where you have been or might be most challenged to make decisions that would infringe on the liberties and independence of your patient? Are you prepared to make them?

_____

_____

_____

_____

_____

_____

_____

~ ☙ ~

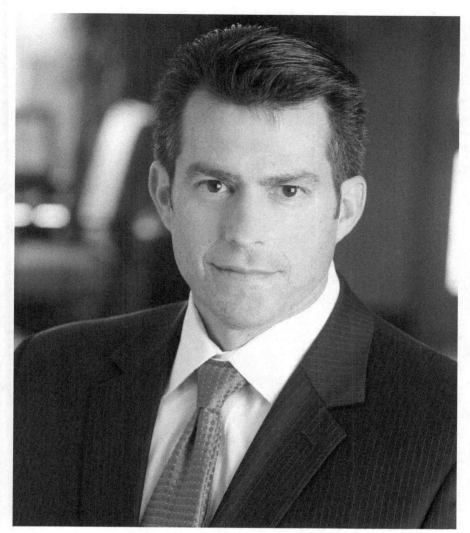

As I've indicated previously, one of Daran's strengths is context. He likes to look back to plan for the future. This photo was a professional headshot taken a couple of years after his cancer recovery. It shows no signs of the impact of those tortuous, not so distant times.

The Space to Define Life's New Chapter

ℰ Key Battle Strategy

Re-Set Expectations

You may note that I have used the word *recovery* respective of Daran's stroke a limited amount throughout this book. That is intentional because the definition of that word has evolved for me throughout the many months post-stroke.

As I mentioned, we are blessed with a vast and varied support network — some we know quite intimately, others are more acquaintances. In the latter part of Daran's inpatient treatment, one of our newer friends contacted me to volunteer his mother's assistance. You see, his mother is a retired speech pathologist.

Due to the holidays and coordination of calendars, she and I couldn't connect until four weeks or so after Daran was released. I spoke with her via phone for a few hours one Saturday morning. That visit came at exactly the right time and significantly impacted my perspective.

Prior to that conversation, I envisioned that Daran would return to being Daran. To her credit and candor, she was kind but still advised me that I was approaching it all wrong.

She told me directly that Daran would never be who he was before the stroke and that it was not fair to him to set that as a benchmark. She pointed out that Daran is forever changed, just as I am forever changed by the stroke.

She then asked, "Can you give him the freedom to become whomever he wants to be next?"

That one question blew everything wide open! It released my expectations so that I could, in turn, offer him that new perspective.

Daran appreciates knowing that we will continue to celebrate his successes, no matter who he becomes next, or however long it takes.

_____

_____

_____

_____

_____

_____

_____

_____

✿ Care Coach Question

How are you changed by your patient's illness? How is your patient affected? What measures can you take to allow yourselves to become the people that you will be next?

_____

_____

_____

_____

_____

_____

_____

_____

Before his cancer diagnosis, I never knew the significance that ringing a bell has for designating the completion of a milestone. In these photos, we document the final stages of Daran's cancer radiation treatment (top photo), as well as post-stroke inpatient rehabilitation therapy (bottom photo). Suffice it to say that we have had enough bell ringing for a lifetime!

Speaking of celebrations, I can't emphasize enough how important it is to celebrate (even in smaller ways) and to celebrate as often as you can. As I mentioned earlier, during Daran's cancer program, we looked for milestone opportunities to commemorate the little victories and then celebrated in a big way by going to Hawaii once we learned that he was cancer-free.

Celebrations became even more important throughout his post-stroke recovery.

For instance, I discreetly planned for a small group of family, including Daran's mom, his son, Scotty, and our brother-in-law, to travel to Houston for his 49th birthday, a little more than two months post-stroke. I coordinated it in such a way that his guests didn't startle him by arriving all at the same time. Instead, he was surprised each time he opened our home's front door and a new loved one was on the other side. It was such a beautiful weekend honoring and loving on him.

Once the coronavirus crisis is over, we are also anticipating a celebration party to thank our friends for their support. While it may not occur this year, we are taking our time to gauge public safety, as well as Daran's ability to be in larger groups again, and will then plan accordingly.

We are also looking forward to traveling again when the time is right. Our philosophy has previously been to book a trip when we're on a trip so that our sights are never far from travel. While they are all special, the next one, no matter when it occurs, will be extraordinary. We just have to get on the other side of this pandemic first!

_____

_____

_____

_____

_____

_____

Care Coach Question

What are you and your patient looking forward to? Are you taking the time to celebrate?

_____

_____

_____

_____

_____

_____

_____

After Daran had completed all treatments and we had received the news that Daran was cancer-free, he asked where we should go that year for our anniversary trip. I told him that we should travel to Hawaii because if any person deserved a trip like that, it was Daran. He agreed. These photos capture a few of our favorite memories from that trip.

Everyone loves a good comeback story and Daran's will be one for the record books. God continues to perform miracles for us through prayers, love, and support.

As I write this, we are more than ten months post-stroke. Several weeks ago, I asked Daran what stands out most regarding the way that I have handled his care.

He told me that it was great how I realized early on that he was going to make mistakes. He appreciates how I allow him to make those mistakes without correcting him. He told me, "You're doing a great job."

For me, that makes it all worthwhile and then some.

We have been working to define our new chapter. We are both okay in knowing that neither of us will ever be who we were before. Too much of life has transpired in the past months, a different intensity of life than we experienced before his stroke.

We are not the same people. Both our spiritual and physical armors have been forged through the fires we have walked through. I am so proud that when tested, we didn't lose faith or hope. No, we dug our heels in and B-E-L-I-E-V-E-D!

We are better, even stronger, from these experiences. Now, we can be a resource and serve others. I pray the same for you, now and always.

_____

_____

_____

_____

_____

_____

_____

☙ *Care Coach Question*

Are you keeping hope alive in your patient? If they lose faith in God and themselves, they will succumb to their battle.

_____

_____

_____

_____

_____

_____

_____

I have used photos to tell our twenty-one+ year history throughout this book. I hope that you have enjoyed getting to know us and our journey a little better in this manner. Here are a few more photos, with more to come in the beautiful future that we are building. Stay tuned...

180 ✢

Summary

As I mentioned earlier, my brain is wired to naturally amass and then distribute a large collection of knowledge. It's the same way with my writing. I know that I have provided a lot of information in this book. However, I have distilled for you the most important concepts below.

The Top 10 Key Battle Strategies for Care Coaches:

1) Surrender

- Are you asking God for *manna* for the day?

- Are you worrying before it's time to worry?

2) Self-Preservation

- What are you doing for you? What are your coping mechanisms?

- Is that inner voice being nice and loving to you?

- Are you people pleasing too much?

3) Pick an Ally and Partner for Battle

- Who are your one or two (max) allies for the battles?

- What are their defined roles (and boundaries) for assisting you?

4) Extract Your Ego to Allow Others to Help You

- Can you ask for help? If not, why?

- Do you have an updated personal communication distribution list as a means to rally those folks closest to you?

- How can you personalize this distribution list to utilize the strengths, talents, and availability of your family and friends who wish to volunteer?

5) Individualize a Program for Your Patient, Yourself, and Your Relationship

- What does a customized program that inspires and motivates him/her look like?

- Can you define one that best leverages your strengths and your relationship?

6) Coaching Your Patient

- Have you determined the boundaries for encouraging and motivating your patient?

- Can you extract your ego to identify and respect the areas in which your patient has set limits?

- Have you articulated your commitment to be with your patient for the long haul?

7) Organization

- Do you know or have a system in place to capture your patient's detailed medical history, medications, current symptoms, and issues if they can't articulate this information for themselves?

- Are you mentally and emotionally prepared to be a patient advocate on behalf of your patient, ready and willing to make all the life or death decisions?

8) Advanced Prep

- Do you have an executed will with financial and medical powers of attorney listing you as the decision-maker?

- Do you know all your patient's usernames and passwords?

- Do you also have knowledge of and access to all their financial accounts and records?

9) Celebrations

- What can you do to honor the important milestones and achievements throughout your patient's program?

- If there is nothing to celebrate (yet), what can you do to laugh despite the challenges?

10) Keeping the Faith

- Who can you call upon as a prayer warrior when you're exhausted and have no more words for prayers?

- What are God's Memorial Stones in which, but for His Goodness, you wouldn't be here? Can you identify three areas to stand in gratitude?

There are a few certain things in life, and one is that change is inevitable. By learning to surrender to today's Grace, I have faith and trust that each challenging season too shall pass. Just as God's Provision and Favor surrounded us in the past, it will be steadfast in the future.

I am blessed to have walked through these trials with God by my side. For that reason, I heard His Calling in obedience to provide encouragement and motivation through our stories. I hope that our blessings will inspire others in their journeys.

Daran has experienced that same beckoning by God. We are beginning to work on a patient memoir which will share his perspective of walking this voyage to health. His documentation will address one of the most common questions that many people have during challenging times, "Why or Why me?"

When I recently asked him this, Daran commented how that question has never occurred to him. He says that looking at it in that manner would be from a victim mentality and that it would be a waste of his time and energy. Daran instead asks, "How can God use this?"

Daran has a faith in God and himself that embodies the warrior armoring up for battle. We look forward to sharing it with you soon. In the meantime, we pray that God continues to Bless and Keep you, now and always.

And there's one last but very important lesson to share with you. Never part from your special person without sharing a kiss and saying "I love you", even if it means doing so many times per day.

You don't know when it might be the last time you hear those words or experience that embrace. Never take a single one for granted!

My Gratitude Journey

I write this as a reminder to you. If you can say that there is *nothing new* to report, then enjoy the place you're in right now. Love on those close to you and never take a moment for granted.

So many factors had to align correctly for us to successfully be where we are today. I am grateful for each and every one of these blessings, and more...

I am grateful for:

- Our Lord for His Healing, Grace, Glory, and Favor.

- Daran's warrior determination to never give up.

- All the previous trials that armored me for the storms of life thus far.

- Generations of prayers from our parents (our mothers, Janice and Annette, especially), grandparents, great grandparents, etc.

- Our forevermore binding thread, *go-to* team of Scotty, Holly, and Randy.

- All the love, prayers, and support for us from family and friends near and far, even when we did not know that we needed it. God spoke to all of them to bless us during times we most needed it. We trust, through our prayers, that God will continue to bless and magnify them.

  - To our close, immediate family including Daran's son, Laine, our brothers-in-law, Michael and Chad, our nieces, Reagan, Juliana and Helen, and nephews, Connor and Carter. Plus, our large and loving Fontenot and Landry extended family, especially Scotty's wife, Shawntel, and their children, Cali, Alyssa and Lyle, for sharing their husband and father with us.

  - To our wonderful friends who have become our family, especially all of those in Houston who held us up and sustained us post-stroke.

  - To my 4word Bible Study Sisters in Christ for their constant love, encouragement, and prayers.

- The vast and varied members of Daran's medical team at MD Anderson, Memorial Hermann and the Mischer Neuroscience Institute, UT Neuroscience, TIRR Memorial Hermann Rehabilitation – Inpatient and Outpatient (especially speech pathologist, Lindsey Duckworth), Village Family Practice (especially Dr. Brent Reed, General Practitioner), as well as the myriad of other physicians, nurses, therapists, paramedics, pharmacists, and their support teams.

- Our fantastic insurance broker (Nadia Troutenko) and Blue Cross Blue Shield for their abiding service to us.

- Our previous and current employers, as well as our clients and allies, for sticking with us, through the good and bad times. We are appreciative for their loyalty and support.

- We are ever so thankful that Daran's stroke occurred during the time that it did and not during the COVID-19 crisis. He had just completed each of his first rounds of follow up doctors' appointments in the weeks just prior to the shutdown of the United States due to the pandemic. We hunkered down and stayed healthy at home during that time.

- For today, because each second, minute, and hour means that Daran is closer to his full and miraculous healing as he begins the new chapter in his life.

- For the beauty of Daran and our loving relationship, partnering friendship, and our faith in God. Our marriage becomes even more strongly bonded as our armor is forged stronger through the fires.

Acknowledgments

- My big dream of writing a book could not be accomplished without a dream book team. *ARMORED's* creative collaborators of design and content artists include Rana Severs, Reagan Simon, and Alyssa Curry. Words cannot express my gratitude for your diligence and hard work in helping to make my dream come true!

- I wish to express additional appreciation to Michelle Prince for being the spark to advise and coach my book writing process and Joann O'Neil for her professional editing services. Additionally, I appreciate the counsel of SCORE mentors Willy Verbrugghe, Toby Haberkorn, and Clark Martin.

- Friends who walked with us through these fiery trials and assisted me to capture, edit, and celebrate this testimonial of God's Grace and Goodness include: Brandi McDonald-Sikes, Tana Deshayes, Lisa and Marshall Martin, Saba Abashawl, Cheryl and Ronnie Gajeske, Mark and Tracy Mitchell, Henry Hagendorf and Beth Young, Elizabeth and Ryan Huff, Dianne Murata and Robb Bunge, John Hunter, Matt Braly, Kenny Barhanovich, Alejandro and Lolita Colom, Oscar Gutierrez, Mark Story, James Rush, Edward de los Angeles, Freddie

and Gloria Bustillo, Sofia Hernandez, Sarah Pellegrin, Marty
Lundstrom, Ali Dupnik, Susan Boyle and Jim Zeveney, Sofia
Fonseca, Raylena Browning, Tina and Mitja Peterman, Denna
and Victor Arias, Diana Davis, Kim Barrow, Jennifer Gonzales,
Laura and Dudley Van Ness, Amy Moen, Jill Pearsall, Charles
and Michele Davis, Stephen LeJeune and Taavi Mark, Melanie
Herz Promecene, Kristin Rickett, Cindy Young, Doug Parker,
Ellary and Dave Makuch, Susan Kramer, Kim Kaase, David
Ladewig, Alex and Brian Phillips, Jon and MJ Moreau, Carlos
and Millie Garza, Steve and Laurie Mechler, David Spaw
and Kimberly Hickson, Ed Slaback, Kurt Nederveld, Paul
Otheguy, Mary Elizabeth and Roger Merrill, Ken Jones, Bob
and Dixie Evans, Andrew Rocha, Craig and Julie Russell,
Michael and Sheila Ballases, Mark and Stacy Courville, Bonnie
Purvis, Kristin Kautz, Margaret and Daniel Mills, Lilly Chu,
Leigh Ann and Gary Henderson, Jamie Elmore-Kelly, Jeanne
Jullien, Heidi Andrews, Sara Collins, LaKeta Morris, Kathleen
Margolis, Maurice and Jeanne LaMontagne, Casey Dubbelde,
Mark Crippen and Nicki Praiswater, Melanie Bean McMurtry,
Patti Miller, Michelle and Brant Perry, Eric and Shari Kruger,
Roberta Bentley, Eddie Garcia, Yvonne Nagy, Lisa Osborne,
Tom Derrah, Jim Kollaer, Cindy Roth, Jennifer Youssef, Joe
Esch, Dr. Mary Ann Reynolds Wilkins, Sharon Steinberg,
Robbin Colgrove, Mary McNair and David Novelli, Mary Le
and Mo Elkurdi, Stephanie Wiggins, Karen Gregory, Ellen
Svestad, Frank Marquez, Sue Jacobson, Regina and Vincent
Morales, Dan Gilbane, Phuc Dang, Juan Polanco, Tonya
Knauth, Siraj Popatia, Raquel Olivier, John Hays Compton,
Chris Fields, Dr. Paula Batterton, and Ken and Joy Fontenot.

- Reflecting upon my past, I would like to state my deepest and most heartfelt gratitude for my professional mentors Cheryl Taylor Bowie, Pam Lovett, Sharon Beadle Smith, as well as my Public Relations Advisor, Dr. Virginia Cromwell. Each of you is the epitome of grace under fire personified. I am so thankful to have you as a role model so early in my career. I would also like to thank my psychologist from so many decades ago, Sidney Creaghan. You will never know the full impact that you had on this formerly lost girl's future and your role in my happiness for a lifetime.

- Finally and not least, I would like to thank my ever-enduring supportive sisterhood including Darlene Fontenot, Amanda Peré Gooch, Angela Pecorino Etheridge, Tiffany Moreno, and Margaret Pering. Little did you know when we became friends so many decades ago that I wouldn't let you go for life!

Note: The hazard in naming a few is that invariably, you may forget someone who helped in the process. Please know how much I appreciate all who helped — past, present, and future...

References and Lagniappe
(a Little Something Extra)

Chapter Two Page 17

- For information about Garth Brooks' song "Unanswered Prayers" – www.garthbrooks.com/music/no-fences

Chapter Two Page 18

- To learn more about Urban Cowboy's "Lookin' for Love" – www.imdb.com/title/tt0081696/soundtrack

Chapter Two Page 19

- For information about HBO's *Sex and the City* – www.imdb.com/title/tt0159206/

Chapter Two Page 27

- For information about *My Big, Fat Greek Wedding* – www.imdb.com/title/tt0259446/

Chapter Three Page 39

- For information about Guillain-Barre' syndrome – www.cdc.gov/campylobacter/guillain-barre.html

Chapter Three Page 39

- For the Mayo Clinic definition of plasmapheresis – www.mayoclinic.org/diseases-conditions/guillain-barre-syndrome/diagnosis-treatment/drc-20363006

Chapter Three Page 43

- For information about head and neck cancer – www.cancer.gov/types/head-and-neck/head-neck-fact-sheet

Chapter Three Page 46

- For information about the UT MD Anderson Cancer Center and its head and neck department – www.mdanderson.org/patients-family/diagnosis-treatment/care-centers-clinics/head-neck-center.html

Chapter Three Page 62

- To identify the signs and symptoms of a stroke – www.stroke.org/en/about-stroke/stroke-symptoms

Chapter Three Page 63

- For information about the Mischer Neuroscience Institute at Memorial Hermann – www.neuro.memorialhermann.org/

Chapter Three Page 71

- My prayer over Daran throughout the day was: "Father, we know that you are Jehovah Rapha, Our Healer. We stand in faith that you have the power to heal Daran from the top of his head to the tips of his toes; and that Daran's cells will be regenerated to their original factory settings as from his mother's womb. We've seen you move mountains on our behalf in the past and know that you will do it again in the future. In Jesus' Name, we pray. Amen."

Chapter Four Page 85

- For information about IZ's "Somewhere Over the Rainbow" – www.izhawaii.com/

Chapter Four Page 87

- For information about *The Marvelous Mrs. Maisel* – www.imdb.com/title/tt5788792/

Chapter Four Page 99

- Access the Medical Chart Anatomy Graphic – www.dawnflandry.com

Chapter Five Page 112

- For information about the Hans Brinker story about the "Dutch Boy and the Dike" – https://en.wikipedia.org/wiki/Hans_Brinker,_or_The_Silver_Skates

Chapter Five Page 120

- Michael Singer's *Surrender Experiment* Information – www.untetheredsoul.com/

Chapter Five Page 134

- For information about the Lotsa app – www.lotsahelpinghands.com/

Chapter Five Page 134

- For information about the TIRR Memorial Hermann Rehabilitation Facility – www.tirr.memorialhermann.org/

Chapter Five Page 138

- For information about Dorothy and her ruby slippers – www.imdb.com/title/tt0032138/

Chapter Five Page 142

- For information about the 4word Bible study –
  www.4wordwomen.org

Chapter Six Page 167

- For information about help and support for depression and/
  or suicide prevention – www.nimh.nih.gov/health/topics/
  suicide-prevention/index.shtml

Chapter Seven Page 181 and Dedication Page xii

- Photography credit by Robyn Arouty. For more details, visit:
  www.robynarouty.com/

About the Author

Dawn F. Landry lives in Houston, Texas with her loving husband, Daran. They are passionate animal lovers and share their home with their third generation of rescued pups. Dawn is a *big dreamer* with a strong faith in surrendering to God's Will. She loves to travel and experience new cultures, and she is also a passionate appreciator and collector of art.

When not being an unintentional care coach, Dawn is an award-winning and respected business professional, working with clients throughout Texas. She has spent the bulk of her twenty-seven-year-career in Houston's corporate real estate industry, excelling in business development and marketing leadership positions within the region's largest economic development organization, as well as international commercial construction companies.

In February 2017, Dawn founded Authentizity, LLC, as an independent business growth strategist to assist companies with customized programs designed to advance their leadership proficiencies, team alignment, and outreach effectiveness. She became a Gallup-Certified CliftonStrengths® Coach and then leveraged that tool to provide consulting, training, and coaching services that optimize technical teams' engagement and productivity.

Little did she know that she would have to tap into all her professional and personal skills as Daran traversed several terminal health battles in their twenty-one+ year, lovingly devoted relationship...

CPSIA information can be obtained
at www.ICGtesting.com
Printed in the USA
JSHW040346051020
8386JS00003B/5

9 781735 354033